WEST MI⎯
RIVER (
FOR CANOEISTS

BRITISH CANOE UNION
WEST MIDLANDS REGION

BY

MIKE NICHOLLS & MIKE HUBBARD

British Library Cataloguing in Publication Data.

A catalogue record for this book is available from the British Library

Published by the British Canoe Union, West Midlands Region
Circa Feb. 1987
2nd edition Oct 1987
3rd edition Feb. 1989
4th edition August 1995

I.S.B.N. No: 0-900082-07-0
LIBRARY CATALOGUE NUMBER: 797.122

The authors would like to thank the following for their help in the preparation of this guide

R. B. Leadley
Birmingham Canoe Club
Walsall College Canoe Club
Anker Valley Canoe Club
North Bromsgrove High School Canoe Club
Sandwell & Dudley Canoe Club
Royal Sutton Coldfield Canoe Club
Shrewsbury Canoe Club
Burton Canoe Club
Drummond Outdoor
Telford Canoe Club
West Midlands Canoe Centre

N.R.A. RIVERLINE

Information about the rivers in the region can be obtained by phoning the following telephone numbers.

TRENT	0891 1122611
AVON/LOWER SEVERN	0891 1122622
MID/UPPER SEVERN (INC VRYNWY)	0891 1122633
WYE	0891 777666

FOREWORD

We are fortunate in the West Midlands Region in that we have a many and varied choice of rivers within easy reach. We have the Fast and technical rivers of the Welsh Borders, but as we go East across the Midland plain we find the rivers quieten down and become slow and rural. Each has it's attractions for the type of paddling we want to do. We also have a great number of canals in the region which can be included in a tour to make a interesting and varied day out for a party of canoeists. There are a great number of very good canal guides in existence and so canals have not been included except as part of a complete tour.

This guide has been produced as a tool to help you plan a days tour on a waterway, you will know your own capabilities, so you can plan to paddle any distance or grade of river you wish. This guide contains most of the land marks along the waterway, possible dangers, access and egress points & also campsites where known. The relevant Ordinance Survey "Landranger" sheet number is included in each guide, these are the ideal maps to compliment the instructions given. The guides in this book will give the access position at a particular location on the waterway concerned, where known. This can change after the book has been printed so if you are challenged, BE POLITE AT ALL TIMES, ascertain the persons authority and afterwards send a report on the incident to the local access officer with a copy to the authors. For the most up to date information on the rivers in this guide send a S.A.E. to the L.C.O. including your B.C.U. number with your enquiry.

Although every effort has been made to make this guide as accurate as possible, the authors cannot be held responsible for any errors, omissions or changes of circumstance contained herein.

Don't just keep on paddling the same old rivers go out and try something new, you will be surprised at the character and variety of some of the smaller rivers in the region, although some of them will require rain to make them worthwhile.

Good Paddling

Mikes

3

The guides in this book are as complete as we can make them at the time of going to press. However, in order to keep the information on our database current we would be pleased to hear from you concerning errors, omissions, alterations or any other information that you found whilst out paddling the rivers of our region.

Please send any new information or alterations to the address below.

M P Nicholls
25 Dunbar Grove
Great Barr
Birmingham
B43 7PT

Please help us to further canoeing in the region.

WATER QUALITY

The National Rivers Authority has a grading systems for water quality in rivers and canals. The code numbers which appear at the head of each guide relate to the key below.

1A   Water of high quality, suitable for potable supply abstractions & capable of supporting game or other high class fisheries.

1B   Water of a less high quality than class 1A but usable for substantially the same purposes.

2   Water suitable for potable supply after advanced treatment, capable of supporting good course fisheries.

3   Water which is polluted to such an extent that fish are absent or sporadically present. May be used for low grade industrial abstraction.

4   Water which is grossly polluted & likely to cause a nuisance.

CONTENTS

RIVER	CANOEABLE LENGTH	PAGE
SEVERN BASIN		
SEVERN	164.5 MILES	8
STOUR	13.1 MILES	15
TERN	16.6 MILES	18
MEESE	N/A MILES	14
REA BROOK	7.5 MILES	20
SALWARPE	7 MILES	22
TEME BASIN		
TEME	67.0 MILES	24
REA	10.8 MILES	30
CLUN	11 MILES	32
ONNY	3.8 MILES	32
AVON BASIN		
AVON	91.5 MILES	34
SOWE	7 MILES	36
STOUR	15.5 MILES	40
LEAM	12.5 MILES	42
ARROW	11 MILES	44
ALNE	3.4 MILES	54
WYE BASIN		
WYE	148.2 MILES	46
ARROW	17.2 MILES	50
LUGG	41.5 MILES	52
TRENT BASIN		
TRENT	50.5 MILES	56
SOW	4 MILES	60
TRENT VALLEY CIRCLES	VARIOUS	61
PENK	18.4 MILES	64
SAREDON BROOK	5.5 MILES	66
ANKER	14.4 MILES	68
REA (B'ham)	6.8 MILES	70
COLE	7.8 MILES	72
TAME	42.5 MILES	74
BLYTHE	11 MILES	88
CHURNET	16.2 MILES	81
DOVE	12.7 MILES	84
MANIFOLD	9.7 MILES	86
HAMPS	4.1 MILES	88

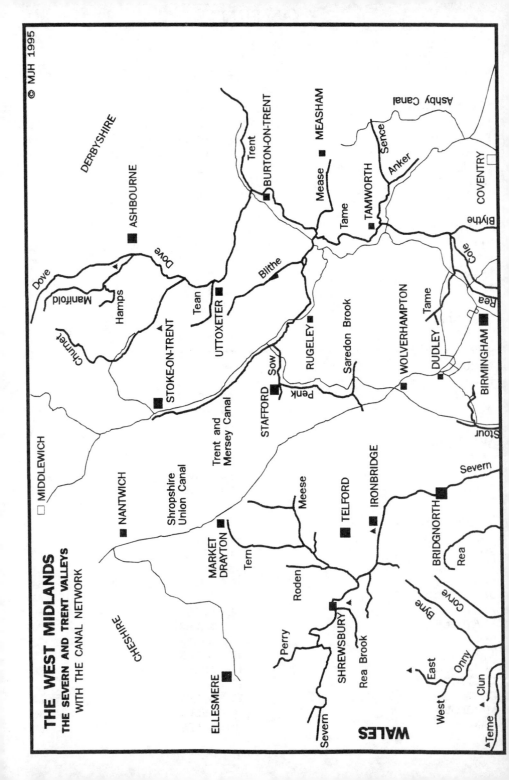

THE WEST MIDLANDS
THE SEVERN AND TRENT VALLEYS
WITH THE CANAL NETWORK

© MJH 1995

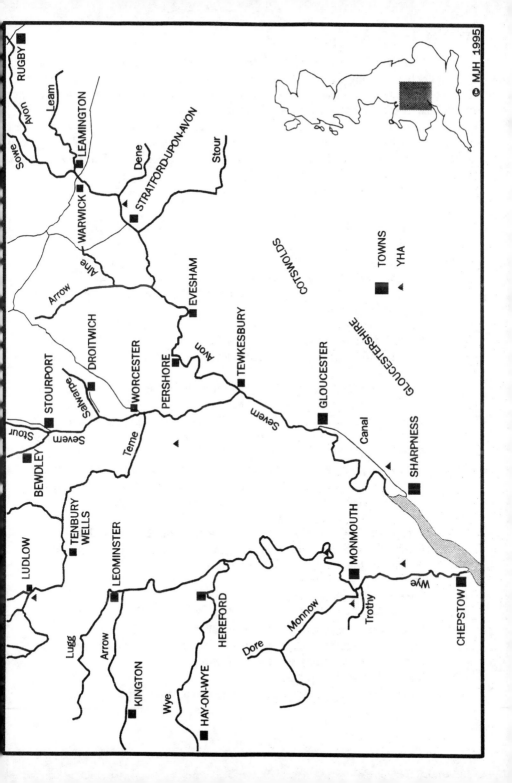

RIVER SEVERN

The river Severn runs off Plynlimon, the highest canoeable point is Geufron in high water but normally it is Llanidloes bridge. The Severn is grade 0/1 but the weirs need inspection in all states. Because there are no weirs between Shrewsbury & Stourport this part of the river is suitable for parties of limited experience.

Access is not normally a problem as many parks, common land & council owned land form it's banks. The river has a public right of navigation from Pool Quay (near Welshpool) to Stourport from where it comes under the control of British Waterways. Campsites are mentioned but most farmers are willing to allow camping but permission must be sought before setting up.

N.R.A. RATING 1B   O/S MAP Nos: 126/7, 138, 162

MILES
59.5   Melverly, confluence with the river Vrynwy, Crew Green bridge SJ 328158
62   Royal Hill Inn, access through campsite, Mrs Pugh, Royal Hill Inn, SY10 8ES
        TEL: 01743 741242
65.5   Shrawardine, island, go left in low water.
68   Montford islands, go either side of first island, then to the right of the second.
69.5   New Montford bridge, (A5). Access downstream right of bridge. Car park,
        picnic site, toilets.
69.7   Old Montford bridge, access, left bank after the bridge through the campsite by
        prior arrangement with the owner, Mr Simmons, Severn House Campsite,
        Montford Bridge, SY4 1ED. TEL: 01743-850-229. Camping also at the
        Wingfield Arms, Montford Bridge, Mr Warner-Smith, TEL: 01743 850750
71   River Perry joins from the left, rapid after.
72.3   Isle Grange, the river flows for almost 5 miles around the isle but to portage
        across the neck it is just 300 metres. Permission to portage must be obtained
        from Isle Grange Farm, near Bicton, Shropshire.
77.8   Portage access from 72.3 miles.
80   Shropshire & West Midlands Show Ground, Coton Hall public slipway, left.
81.3   Frankwell footbridge, canoe launching ramp after the bridge. Camping contact
        Drummond Outdoor, TEL: 01743 365022
81.4   Shrewsbury, Welsh bridge.
81.7   Footbridge, boathouses just downstream.
82.1   Toll bridge.
82.5   Footbridge, Shrewsbury Youth Hostel half a mile.
82.7   Shrewsbury, English bridge, Rea Brook joins from the right just before the
        bridge (see separate chapter also for Y.H.A.).
82.9   Shrewsbury Station bridge.
83.1   Footbridge. Drummond Outdoor, centre on the downstream left bank.

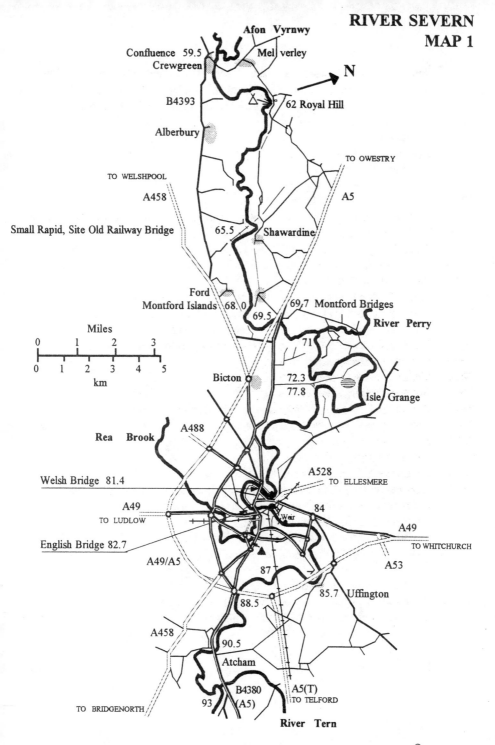

RIVER SEVERN
MAP 1

Afon Vyrnwy

Confluence 59.5
Crewgreen

Mel verley

N

B4393

62 Royal Hill

Alberbury

TO OWESTRY

TO WELSHPOOL

A458

A5

Small Rapid, Site Old Railway Bridge

65.5

Shawardine

Ford
Montford Islands 68.0

69.7 Montford Bridges

69.5

River Perry

Miles

71

0   1   2   3

0   1   2   3   4   5

km

72.3

Bicton

77.8

Isle Grange

Rea   Brook

A488

Welsh Bridge 81.4

A528

TO ELLESMERE

A49

84

TO LUDLOW

Weir

A49

TO WHITCHURCH

English Bridge 82.7

A49/A5

A53

87

85.7 Uffington

88.5

A458

90.5

Atcham

B4380

A5(T)

TO TELFORD

TO BRIDGENORTH

93

(A5)

River Tern

9

© MJH 1995

83.3	Shrewsbury weir, portage left, launch from canoe ramp, left side for med/high water, right side low water only. The weir has a large tow back in high water but there is a break in the stopper at the left end. It is advisable to inspect always.
84	Telford way bridge, (A49).
84.9	By-pass bridge, (A49).
85.7	By-pass bridge, (A49).
87	Belvedere Railway bridge.
88,5	By-pass bridge, (A5 & A49).
89.3	Chilton Island, go left hand side.
90.5	Atcham Bridges, (B4390), go through centre arch of bridges. Access from right bank after second bridge. Shop & pub.
93	River Tern joins from the left, (see Tern chapter).
93.8	Wroxeter, site of Roman ruins, access left of the islands.
95.3	Cound Brook joins from the right.
96	Cound Lodge Inn on the right. Camping, TEL: 01952 510322.
98.3	Cressage bridge, (B4380), access just before the bridge left bank. Over the next five miles the river meanders with many shallows and shingle banks in low water.
103.3	Buildwas bridge, (A4169), no access here, power station on the right.
104.1	Bridge, private to power station.
104.3	Bridge, private to power station.
104.4	Railway bridge (Albert Edward).
104.5	Ironbridge Rowing club steps on the left, access through park.
104.7	Dale End Park, Access left bank, toilets, Coalbrookdale Museum, town, shops.
105.5	Ironbridge, the worlds first iron bridge, town on the left.
106	New Free Bridge, (B4373).
106.2	Ironbridge Y.H.A. right bank.
106.3	Jackfield rapid, 170 metres grade 1/2 rapid, channel on the right through standing waves. Access/egress/camping by prior arrangement only from secretary, Telford Canoe Club.
107.1	The Boat Inn, footbridge, Blists Hill industrial museum on the left.
107.5	Coalport bridge. Camping, Woodbridge TEL: 01952 882054
110.5	Apley bridge, private.
113.1	River Worfe joins from the left.
114.3	Bridgnorth Rowing Club steps, access from car park left.
114.5	Bridgnorth bridge, town & Severn Valley railway on the right.
115	Bridgnorth by-pass bridge, (A458).
120	Pipe bridge.

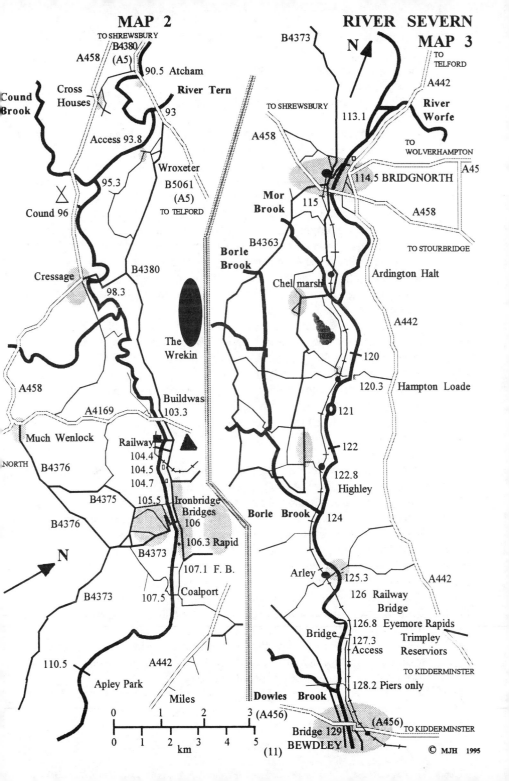

MAP 2

TO SHREWSBURY
B4380
A458 (A5)
90.5 Atcham
Cross
Houses
River Tern
Cound
Brook
93
Access 93.8
Wroxeter
95.3
B5061
(A5)
TO TELFORD
Cound 96
Cressage
B4380
98.3
The
Wrekin
A458
Buildwas
A4169
103.3
Much Wenlock
Railway
NORTH
B4376
104.4
104.5
104.7
B4375
105.5
Ironbridge
Bridges
106
B4376
106.3 Rapid
N
B4373
107.1 F. B.
Coalport
B4373
107.5
110.5
A442
Apley Park
Miles

RIVER SEVERN
MAP 3

B4373
N
TO
TELFORD
A442
TO SHREWSBURY
113.1
River
Worfe
A458
TO
WOLVERHAMPTON
A45
114.5 BRIDGNORTH
Mor
Brook
115
A458
B4363
TO STOURBRIDGE
Borle
Brook
Ardington Halt
Chel marsh
A442
120
120.3 Hampton Loade
121
122
122.8
Highley
Borle Brook
124
Arley
125.3
A442
126 Railway
Bridge
126.8 Eyemore Rapids
Bridge
Trimpley
127.3
Reservoirs
Access
TO KIDDERMINSTER
128.2 Piers only
Dowles Brook
0   1   2   3 (A456)
(A456)
TO KIDDERMINSTER
0   1   2   3   4   5
Bridge 129
km
(11)
BEWDLEY
© MJH 1995

120.3	Hampton Loade, ferry, access from car park left bank. Camping, Unicorn Inn TEL: 01746 861515.
121	Island, go either side but right side is more interesting.
122	Alverly Colliery bridge, private.
122.8	Highley, access right bank by the inn, camping.
124	Borle Brook joins from the right.
125.3	Arley, footbridge, access from both banks (old ferry landings) . Car park/toilets left bank, inns, shop, car park on right bank also.
126	Railway bridge (Victoria), shingle bank after go left.
126.8	Eyemore rapid, grade 1 the last natural rapid on the river, left of the island.
127	Rock ledge, shoot on the right in low water.
127.3	Pipe bridge, access up steps downstream left bank into small car park at the end off Rag Lane (turn right just before garage after railway bridge in Bewdley).
128.2	Dowles bridge, (piers only standing). Dowles Brook joins from the right, this brook has been canoed from Brand Wood in spate but the footpath bridge at the confluence will be at water level and will need portaging.
129	Bewdley bridge, town on the right, access 200 metres before the bridge on the right into pay & display car park.
129.1	Access into pay & display car park at the end of the quay right bank.
129.3	Bewdley Canoe Centre, concrete landing stage on the left bank. Access by prior arrangement from Wyre Forest Canoe Club TEL: 01384 897498.
129.8	Bewdley by-pass bridge, (A456).
130	Blackstone Rock, access right up steep bank after small island into lay-by on B4194, ideal parking out of fishing season.
130.1	River becomes navigable by larger craft.
133	Stourport bridge, (A451), access into dock on the left just after the bridge, car park, town on left.
133.1	Staffordshire & Worcestershire Canal joins from lock gates on the left.
133.4	River Stour joins from behind piling wall on the left.
134.1	Stourport Marina, left bank, services.
134.5	Lincombe weir & lock, shoot 5 metres from right end in low water through standing wave. must be inspected in high water. Portage on the right.
135.6	Dick Brook joins from the right.
138	Lenchford ferry, campsite.
138.8	Holte Fleet weir & lock, shoot only in low water, Salmon ladder can dangerous.
138.9	Holte Fleet bridge, (A443), campsite.
141.6	Grimley, river Salwarpe joins from the left (see Salwarpe chapter), campsite by paddling up the Salwarpe half a mile to Hawford bridge.
142.3	Bevere weir & lock, shoot on the left down salmon ladder, always inspect in high water, portage right. Access off A443 S/P Grimley when entering village turn right down lane, access behind Camp Inn.
145.3	Worcester Canoe Club, Boat house, access from Grandstand Road, Worcester.
145.4	Footbridge.
145.5	Railway bridge.

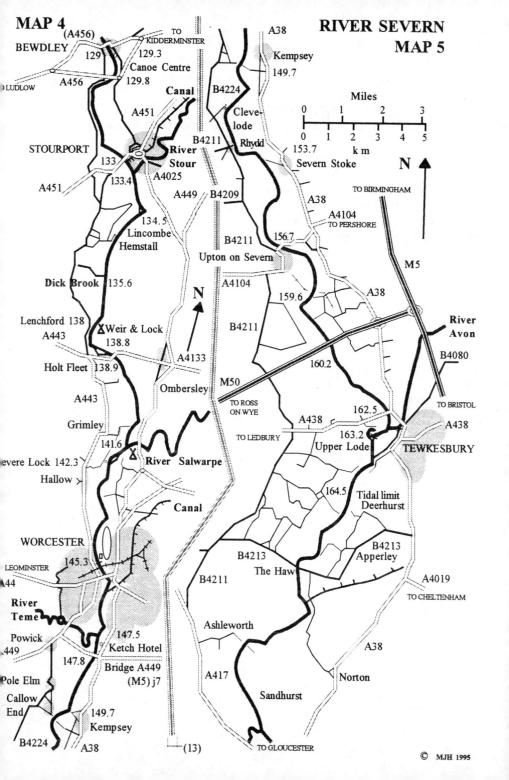

145.8	Worcester bridge, (A44), town & Cathedral on the left.
146.3	Worcester & Birmingham canal joins from the left.
146.8	Diglis weir & lock, shoot in the centre low water only, inspect in med/high water.
147.5	Powick, river Teme joins from the right (see Teme guide).
147.8	Ketch Hotel Bridge, (A449), access under the bridge right bank then across field to gate into lay-by.
156.8	Upton-on-Severn bridge, (A4101), best access just downstream left.
160.3	Queenhill motor way bridge (M50).
162.5	Tewkesbury bridge, (A38), town on left in half a mile.
162.7	River Avon joins from the left, (see Avon guide).
163.2	Upper Lode weir & lock, always inspect weir first.
164.5	The river becomes tidal at this point.

RIVER MEESE

Several streams flow into Aquelate Mere, from which flows the river Meese. It flows in a Westerly direction to join the river Tern (at 5 miles) at Cold Hutton Heath.

RIVER STOUR (WORCESTERSHIRE).

The river Stour runs off the North side of the Clent Hills, it then curves through the Black Country towns of Halesowen, Lye & Stourbridge, after a spell in the country it then passes through Kidderminster to join the river Severn at Stourport.

Knowing the area that it flows through it will come as no surprise that it is very polluted. It has the character of an urban river flowing fast between high vertical banks, rising very fast after rain. In places it is heavily engineered and flows through tunnels under Stourbridge and Kidderminster but in between it takes a meandering course. There are some dangerous obstacles on this river & so the leader must be alert at all times. The river is grade 0/1 in most states.

N.R.A. GRADE 3   O/S MAP Nos: 138/9

MILES

0	Prestwood bridge, (A449), only access from field downstream right of the bridge, ask at nursery first.
0.5	Bridge.
0.7	Aqueduct, Staffs & Worcestershire canal, Smestow Brook joins from right.
1.1	Stewpony weir, shoot centre/left, don't go near the right hand end because of pipework in a cut out in the weir face. This weir is dangerous in high water. ALWAYS INSPECT THIS WEIR.
1.2	Stewpony bridge, (A458), watch for stakes after the bridge.
1.7	Bridge.
2.3	Hyde bridge.
2.4	Footbridge.
3.2	Kinver bridge.
4.1	Farm bridge.
4.2	Portage to canal left bank.
4.3	Highgrove bridge, there are pipes 1metre above summer level on the upstream side of the bridge, there is also a weir on the downstream side of the bridge. ALWAYS INSPECT egress right into the wood 100 metre upstream and portage over the road to launch after the weir on the right. It may be worth the drive to inspect this bridge before the river is attempted.
5.2	Caunsall bridge, the engineered banks by this bridge will make access difficult but not impossible.
5.5	Bridge.
6	Cookley bridge, access from public footpath downstream of the bridge.
7	Bridge.
7.5	Bridge.
7.7	Wolverley bridge, river divides, both routes are possible but the main stream takes the left side. The right route is shallow and goes over a small weir by Wolverley Court Mill.

8	River joins again.
9	Kidderminster, the river flows through a newly constructed supermarket car park before going under the canal and A456 ring road into a deep culvert.
9.5	River divides, DON'T TAKE THE LEFT ROUTE, it is possible but not advisable, GO RIGHT.
10.2	Bridge, small rapid under.
10.3	River joins again, best egress by paddling up the left hand stream for a few metres, this is close to the A451/A449 Stourport Road island, canal is close here also.
10.5	Foley Park viaduct, (Severn Valley Railway). River divides for 800 metres either side of Falling Sands, take right channel.
11.2	Canal close, near to lock.
12.5	Wilden bridge, no egress.
13.5	Bridge.
13.8	Old railway bridge.
14.1	Upper Mitton Bridge, rapid under.
14.5	Old railway bridge.
14.6	Bridge.
14.7	Bridge, (A4025), small rapid under.
15.1	Confluence with the river Severn at 133.4 miles. This may not be immediately noticeable as there is a large piling wall erected as a flow control measure, you will have to paddle between it and the wall of the old power station for 100 metres before emerging onto the river Severn. Egress in 300 metres left bank by the old dock, road access through the Marina Industrial Estate.

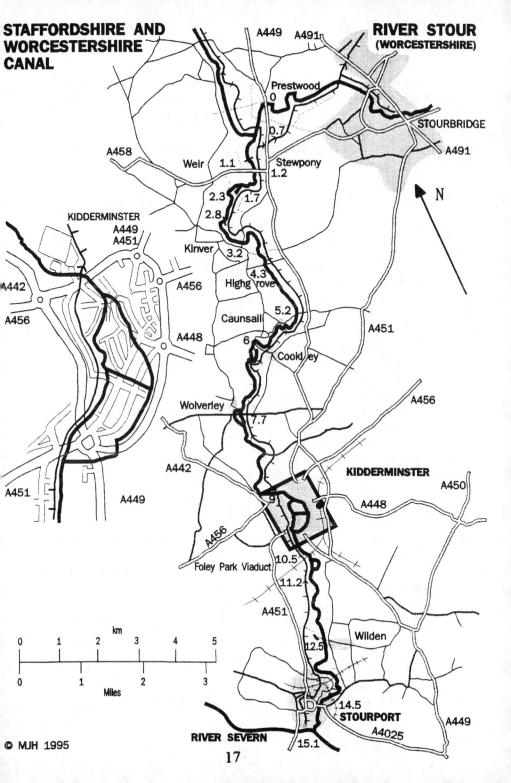

STAFFORDSHIRE AND WORCESTERSHIRE CANAL

RIVER STOUR
(WORCESTERSHIRE)

A449 A491

Prestwood
0

STOURBRIDGE

0.7

A491

A458

Weir 1.1 Stewpony
1.2

N

2.3 1.7

2.8

KIDDERMINSTER
A449
A451

Kinver 3.2

A456 Highgrove 4.3

A442

Caunsall 5.2

A456

A448 6

A451

Cookley

Wolverley 7.7

A456

A442

KIDDERMINSTER A450

9

A448

A456

Foley Park Viaduct 10.5

11.2

A451

Wilden

12.5

14.5

STOURPORT

A4025 A449

RIVER SEVERN 15.1

km
0   1   2   3   4   5

0   1   2   3
Miles

© MJH 1995

17

RIVER TERN

The river Tern flows off Bar Hill by the village of Onneley. It then flows through Market Drayton & skirts Wellington to join the river Severn by Atcham.

The river can be canoed from Stoke-on-tern in flood but in normal water the start is Longdon-on-Tern.

This small river is an easy paddle in most states but some places may need portaging in drought conditions.

N.R.A. GRADE 1B to 12.6 miles, 2 after   **O/S MAP Nos: 126,127**

MILES

0	Stoke-on-Tern bridge.
2	Bridge, this bridge marks the boundary of Ollerton Park, 100 metres after it the river enters the park lake, keep to the right bank for exit right..
2.4	Bridge, the river now leaves the park.
3.2	Eaton Mill, (site 0f).
4	Little Bolas bridge.
5	Cold Hutton Heath, river Meese joins from the left.
6	Waters Upton bridge, (A442), possible access 100 metres upstream.
6.6	Old railway bridge.
7.2	Crudgington bridge, (B5062), confluence of the upper Strine follows.
9	Aqueduct, old Newport branch of Shropshire Union Canal.
9.1	Longdon-on-Tern bridge, (B5063), start point for low water.
9.5	Confluence of the lower Strine
12.6	Walcot Mill weir, this is a new rise & fall weir & must be portaged. The river Roden joins from the right at the end of the weir pool.
12.7	The Lees bridge.
14.1	Railway bridge, followed by road bridge (A5).
15.5	Upton Forge bridge, low bridge.
15.8	Attingham Park bridge, (Nat Trust), permission may be refused to pass through the park, check first.
16.2	Attingham park weir, unshootable due to insufficient depth at the foot, portage left.
16.3	Bridge, (B4380), no access possible here.
16.6	Confluence with the river Severn at 94.3 miles, best egress Wroxeter in 1 mile.

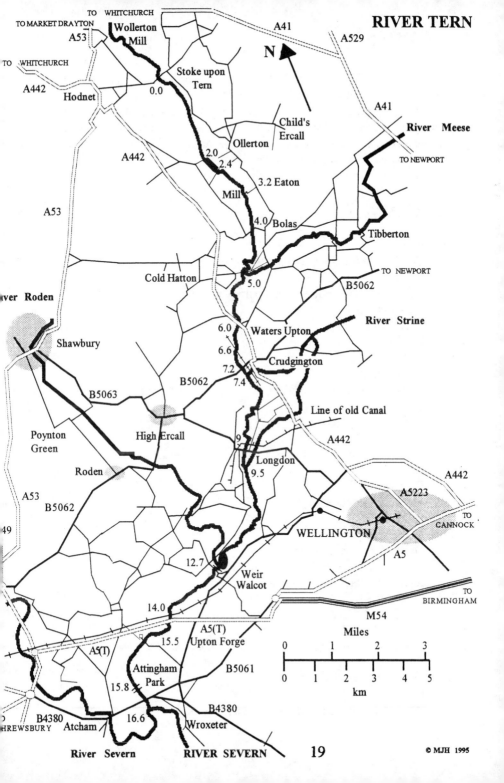

RIVER TERN

REA BROOK

Rea Brook flows out of Marton Pool in a North-easterly direction to join the river Severn by the English bridge in Shrewsbury.

It is a quiet little river with a grade of 0/1, it can be canoed at most times of the year except in a drought. The river is used for open Canadian touring, it also has a slalom site at Rea Brook Estate in Shrewsbury, further details of this can be obtained from R Drummond, 8 Severn Bank, Shrewsbury.

Beware of limited headroom under some bridges in high water.

N.R.A. GRADE 1B   O/S MAP No: 126

MILES

0	Cruckmeole ford, high water start point.
0.2	Bridge.
0.8	Great Hanwood bridges, first a railway bridge followed by a small weir then a road bridge, (A488).
1	Footbridge.
1.2	Bridge.
1.3	Railway bridge.
2.3	Railway bridge.
2.8	Hookagate weir, followed by a bridge, low water start point.
3	Redhill bridge.
3.2	Shrewsbury by-pass bridge, (A5).
3.5	Footbridge.
4	Footbridge, limited clearance, followed by a small weir and a sharp left hand bend.
4.1	Footbridge.
4.5	Meole Brace bridge.
5	Railway bridge.
5.2	Bridge.
5.3	Footbridge, limited clearance.
5.5	Slalom site, followed by a footbridge.
6	Railway bridge, small rapid underneath.
6.2	Footbridge.
6.5	Bridge, (A458). Y.H.A. downstream right.
6.6	Bridge, (A5112).
6.7	Old railway bridge egress just after into public car park right.
6.9	Bridge.
7.1	Railway bridge.
7.3	Bridge.
7.5	Confluence with the river Severn at 84.1 miles.

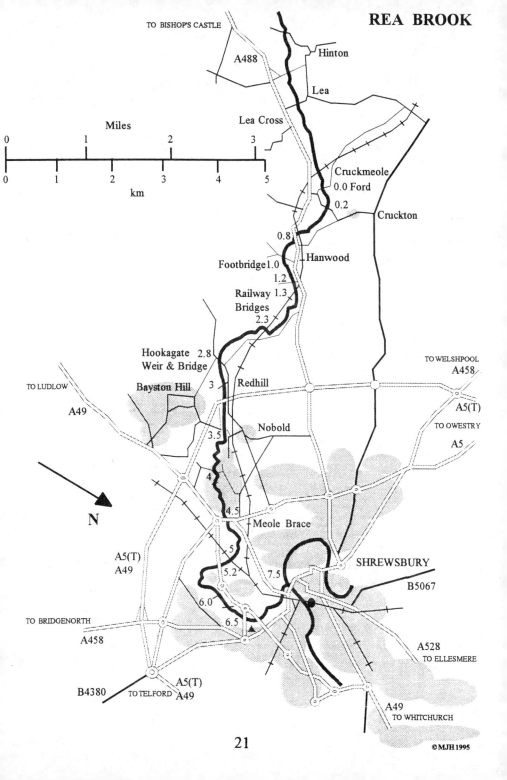

REA BROOK

TO BISHOP'S CASTLE

Hinton

A488

Lea

Lea Cross

Cruckmeole
0.0 Ford
0.2

Cruckton

0.8

Footbridge 1.0
1.2
Railway 1.3
Bridges
2.3

Hanwood

Hookagate 2.8
Weir & Bridge

Bayston Hill   3   Redhill

TO WELSHPOOL
A458

TO LUDLOW
A49

A5(T)

TO OWESTRY
A5

3.5   Nobold

4

4.5   Meole Brace

5

5.2   7.5

SHREWSBURY

B5067

6.0

6.5

A5(T)
A49

TO BRIDGENORTH

A458

A528
TO ELLESMERE

B4380   A5(T)
TO TELFORD   A49

A49
TO WHITCHURCH

Miles
0   1   2   3
0   1   2   3   4   5
km

N

21

© MJH 1995

RIVER SALWARPE

The river Salwarpe rises on Stoney Hill near Bromsgrove & flows towards Droitwich, on the way it is joined by many small streams & so upon reaching Droitwich it becomes canoeable.

It must be said that rain is needed to canoe this river, it is narrow & twisting with a ruling grade of 0/1. It can be littery around Droitwich but improves as it goes out into the country. For most of it's route it is shadowed by the Droitwich canal which is now mostly restored & is navigable from Droitwich town to lock 3. It is in water from lock 5 to the A449 (summer 1995). Permission to paddle the canal can be obtained from Droitwich Canal Trust, TEL: 01905 458352.

N.R.A. RATING 3 to 2 miles, 2 after   O/S MAP NO: 150

MILES

0	Droitwich bridge, (B4090), access by small weir and lock where the canal & river divide.
0.2	Two footbridges.
0.5	Bridges, rail then road.
0.7	Bridge.
0.9	Footbridge.
1.2	Newton bridge, followed by two footbridge.
1.4	Stream joins from the right.
1.9	Bridge.
2	By-pass bridge, (A38).
2.3	Footbridge.
2.4	Salwarpe village bridge.
2.7	Hadley Brook joins from the right followed by footbridge.
3.5	Harford Hill bridge.
4.5	Porters Hill weir & bridge, ALWAYS INSPECT, grating under bridge may be blocked with debris. Portage right.
5.5	Chatley bridge.
6.5	Hawford bridge, (A449), campsite on the left.
7	Confluence with the river Severn at 142.9 miles.

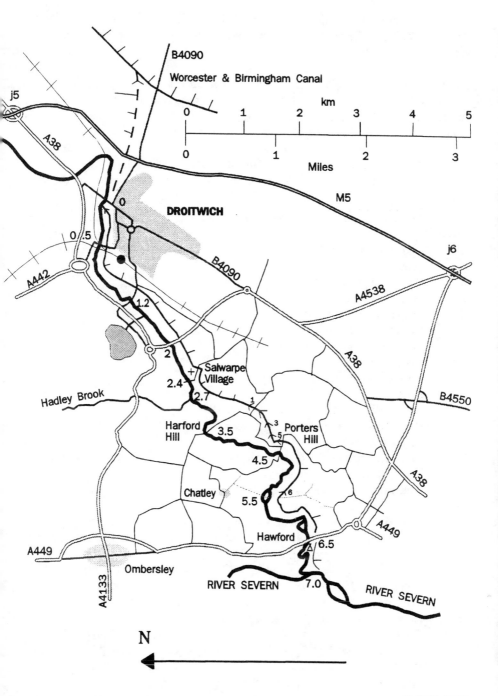

© MJH 1995

RIVER TEME

The river Teme flows off Kerry Hill and flows in a Southerly through Knighton, Ludlow, Tenbury & Martley to join the river Severn at Powick near Worcester.

the river can be canoed from Knighton in spate but the usual starting place is Burrington bridge near Leintwardine. There is currently no access agreement between here & Ludlow so it is important that the L.A.O. is consulted before a tour is planned on this section. After Ludlow there are little or no restrictions & it is a most enjoyable paddle at most times of the year. The river is dotted with mills and their weirs, most can be shot safely but all should be inspected.

The river grading is 2/3 for the Downton Gorge section, 1/2 for the Ludlow to Little Hereford section and 0/1 from here down to the Severn, depending on the levels of water.

N.R.A. RATING 1A TO LUDLOW, THEN 1B

MILES   O/S MAP Nos: 137/8, 150

0	Knighton bridge, village on the right, watch for barbed wire. Y.H.A. hostel temporarily closed 1995.
0.2	Weir by pumping station.
2	Milebrook bridge.
5.5	Lingen bridge, (B4367), and weirs.
6.3	Brampton Brian bridge.
7	Weir, can be portaged on the right.
7.5	Buckton bridge.
8.9	River Clun joins from the left, (see Clun Guide).
9	Leintwardine bridge, (A4110), weir just after can be shot anywhere, village left, Access downstream left.
10.2	Pipe bridge, (Elan Valley to Birmingham).
11	Criftin Ford bridge.
14.2	Burrington bridge, this is the usual start point for the Downton Gorge section, access downstream left bank.
15.3	Pipe bridge, (Elan Valley to Birmingham).
15.7	Bowbridge, old packhorse bridge.
16	Hay Mill weir, this weir is on a sharp right bend, the river is in a gorge just prior to the weir, portage must be made by landing some 200 metres upstream right and carrying round the hill to just by the old mill. The weir is best shot at the extreme right end in all states, paddle along the rock wall and shoot a few metres from the right hand end.
16.6	Broken weir & island, go right of the island to miss the weir.
16.7	Downton Little Castle bridge, castle on the left.
17.5	Bringewood Forge bridge and weir, **THIS WEIR MUST NOT BE SHOT ANY CIRCUMSTANCES,** it has a large mushroom stopper which has caused fatalities in the past. Land in the mouth of the mill stream 150 metres upstream right, Carry round & put in just after the bridge right.

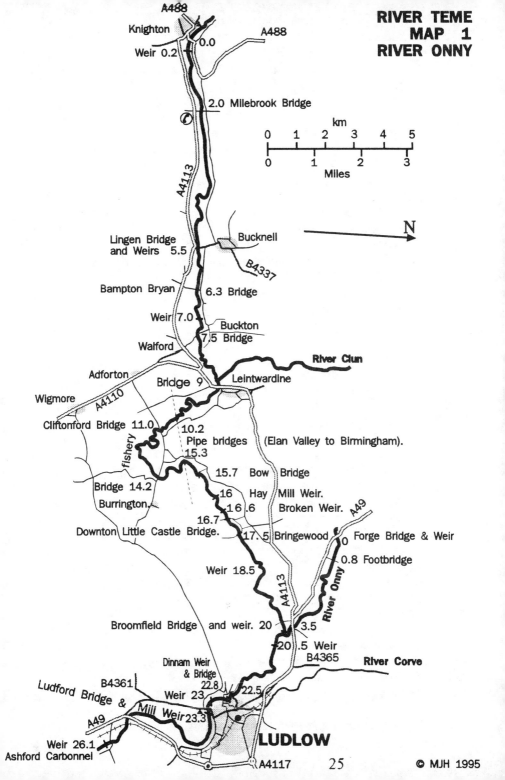

A488

Knighton

A488

Weir 0.2 — 0.0

2.0 Milebrook Bridge

km

0 1 2 3 4 5

0 1 2 3

Miles

N

A4113

Lingen Bridge
and Weirs 5.5

Bucknell

B4337

Bampton Bryan — 6.3 Bridge

Weir 7.0

Buckton
7.5 Bridge

Walford

Adforton

Bridge 9

Leintwardine

River Clun

Wigmore

A4110

Cliftonford Bridge 11.0

10.2

Pipe bridges (Elan Valley to Birmingham).

15.3

fishery

15.7 Bow Bridge

Bridge 14.2

16 Hay Mill Weir.

Burrington

16.6 Broken Weir.

A49

16.7

Downton Little Castle Bridge.

17.5 Bringewood

0 Forge Bridge & Weir

0.8 Footbridge

Weir 18.5

A4113

River Onny

Broomfield Bridge and weir. 20

3.5

20.5 Weir

B4365

River Corve

Dinnam Weir
& Bridge

B4361

22.8

22.5

Ludford Bridge &

Weir 23

A49

Mill Weir 23.3

LUDLOW

Weir 26.1
Ashford Carbonnel

A4117

25

© MJH 1995

18.5	Weir, angled left to right, shoot at far right end.
20	Bromfield bridge and small weir, go through right arch.
20.3	River Onny joins from the left, (see Onny guide).
20.5	Onny weir, rebuilt 1993, inspect before shooting. Can be dangerous in spate.
22.5	River Corve joins from the left.
22.6	Access from Linney recreation ground, toilets & car park (80p per day).
22.7	Dinham weir, shoot centre left in all states, good play spot.
22.8	Dinham bridge, access downstream right from common land.
23	Weir, can be shot in most states, in high water tow back is strong, after the weir go left of the island.
23.3	Ludford bridge, shoot centre or right arch. Y.H.A hostel downstream right.
23.4	Ludford Mill weir, this is a "V" shaped weir with the point facing upstream, the top right corner is broken so the main stream curves left then right ending in a stopper which can be penetrated in most states. Portage over right sill in low water, there is no portage in high water but there is a break at the end of the right sill which can be shot safely in most states. TO AVOID DISTURBING THE LOCAL RESIDENTS PLEASE BE QUIET ON THE RAPID AND IF ASKED TO MOVE ON, DO SO QUICKLY & POLITELY.
23.7	Weir, at an acute angle across the river, ALWAYS INSPECT, THIS WEIR IS IN THE PROCESS OF COLLAPSING AT THE RIGHT END AND SHOULD BE TREATED WITH CAUTION.
23.9	Pipe bridge.
24.2	Pipe bridge, (Elan Valley to Birmingham).
24.5	Small rapid, shoot right in all states.
25.5	Ludlow by-pass bridge, (A49). Access upstream left bank, park well off road.
25.6	Railway bridge.
26	Ashford bridge.
26.1	Ashford Carbonnel weir, this is a curved weir & must be inspected in high water, it can be shot in most states by following a simple rule, shoot centre in low water & on the left in high water. portage left bank. Access by prior arrangement only by telephoning the owner on 0158474 650.
26.3	Beach on right corner, ideal lunch stop.
28	Barrett's Mill, broken weir, go left of island, right side only possible in high water. INSTRUCTORS PLEASE NOTE! The friendly owners of the mill house request that parties do not gather above the old weir (at the bottom of their garden) to receive instructions. Do it higher upstream.
29	Demolished aqueduct, shoot centre, small rapid after.
29.6	Little Hereford bridge, (A456).
30	Little Hereford church and footbridge.
32.3	Bridge, farm road.
32.8	Ledwyche Brook joins from the left, Burford House & gardens on the left.
33.2	Burford weir, 500cm high weir broken on the left.
33.7	Tenbury bridge, (A4112), Access downstream right up slipway car park 20 metres.
36.8	River Rea joins from the left (See Rea guide), small rapid after.

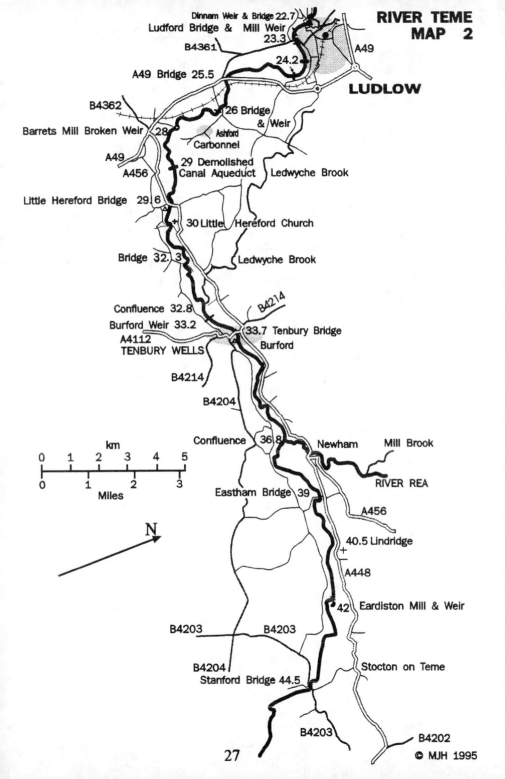

39	Eastham bridge, (just off A443) access after the bridge small car park.
40.5	Lindridge.
42	Eardiston Mill, old low broken weir.
44.5	Stanford bridge, (B4203).
46.5	Shelsey Beauchamp.
47.5	Newmill bridge.
49	Ham bridge, (B4204), lay-by close, access from upstream left bank.
49.7	Ham Mill, site of old weir, small rapid, site used for slaloms.
53.5	Low broken weir, covered in high water.
54.2	Knightwick Mill, small weir, covered in high water.
54.5	Knightsford bridge, Talbot Inn, access up steep bank left into old roadway.
54.7	New Knightsford bridge, (A44), access down steps left lay-by close.
60.5	Liegh Court, church on right, liegh Brook joins from the right.
62.2 the	Bransford bridge, (A4104), access from steps upstream left, small weir after the bridge. From here to the Severn right of passage is contested by local anglers.
62.5	Island, left for main channel, right is possible but narrow.
63	Railway bridge, small rapid under.
65.2	Powick weir, shoot through 4 metre wide gap on the left, there is a large but generally safe standing wave at the foot. It is also possible to go down the mill stream and shoot down the side of the mill wall.
65.3	Powick old bridge.
65.5	Powick new bridge, (A419).
67	Confluence with the river Severn at 148.8 miles, egress in 400 metres on the right under the Ketch bridge, across field into lay-by.

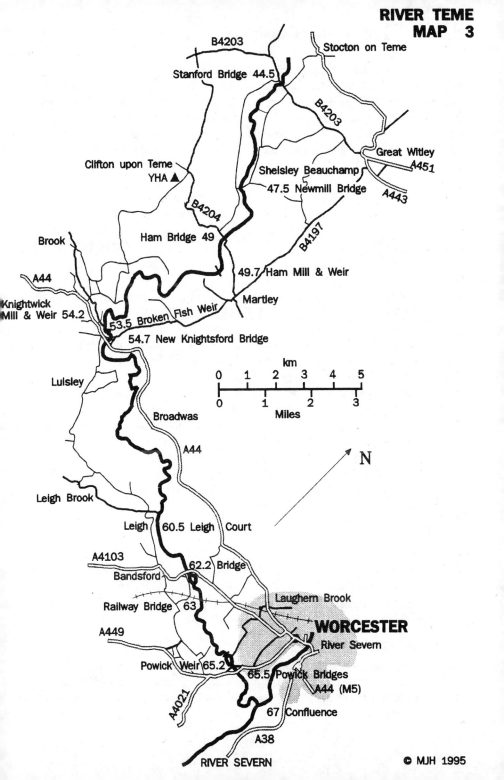

RIVER REA (SHROPSHIRE)

The river Rea runs off Brown Clee Hill near to Ditton Priors, In it's first three miles it is joined by five other streams and by Neen Savage it becomes canoeable in med/high water. It flows thereafter through Cleobury Mortimer, Neen Sollars to join the river Teme by Newnham Bridge. The river is grade 2/3 in high water & grade 2 in medium water. Caught with just the right water it can be memorable tour. There is a water level gauge at Neen Sollars and by following this guide the river level can be estimated.

Water under 63.9 too dry, not worth it.

Water between 64-64.5 river at best level grade 2.

Water over 64.5 unforgettable but can be dangerous.

N.R.A. RATING 1B   O/S MAP No: 138

MILES

0	Neen Savage, access from ford by "T" junction 200 metres after the village, M/R 675.775.Z PLEASE PARK THOUGHTFULLY .
1	Rock fall, 1 metre high near vertical , BEWARE, large tow back in high water, Shoot on left with support in high water. Portage on the left.
1.2	Cleobury Mortimer bridge, (A4117), no access.
2.5	Small falls, 3 falls dropping from pool to pool.
3	Pipe bridge & broken weir, shoot on the right through a gap in the weir, interesting & technical in high water.
4	Weir & ford, usually known as the "Cheesegrater" it is a large weir at least 10 metres long at an angle of 45 degrees. The weir has a ford on top of it so you must first drop over the small lip onto the road & then drop 1 metre onto the weir face and Whee! what a ride! Best approach is to keep left, land and inspect. Shoot left side, sounds big & bad but it's great fun & not very dangerous.
4.7	Nineva bridge.
6.5	Old railway bridge, rapid.
6.8	Footbridge.
7	Neen Sollars bridge, village 200 metres right, egress up bank just before the bridge. Best parking 200 metres left of the bridge down lane. PLEASE PARK THOUGHTFULLY & GET CHANGED DISCREATLY
7.8	Testhill weir, shoot right, sharp bend after the weir.
7.9	Farm bridge.
8.2	Mill Brook joins from the right.
10	Newnham Bridge, (A456), egress either side just before the bridge.
10.2	Weir, shoot on the right, ALWAYS INSPECT, take care in high water.
10.8	Confluence with the river Teme at 36.8 miles, next egress at Eastham bridge in 2.2 miles.

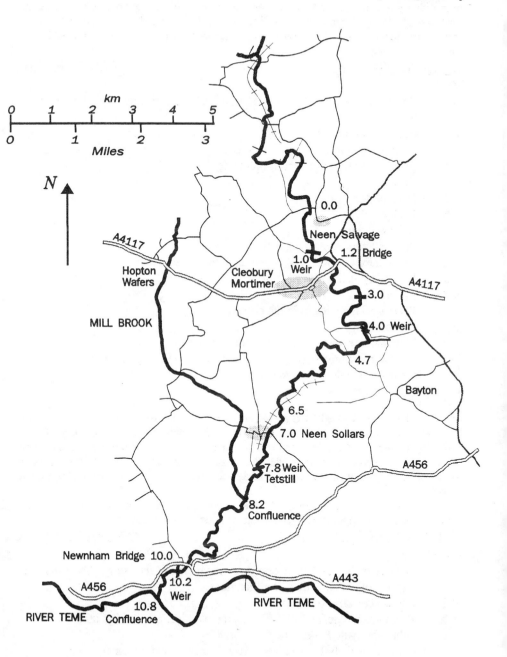

RIVER REA
(Shropshire)

km

0   1   2   3   4   5

0   1   2   3
Miles

N

A4117

Hopton
Wafers

Cleobury
Mortimer

Neen Salvage

0.0

1.2 Bridge

1.0
Weir

A4117

MILL BROOK

3.0

4.0 Weir

4.7

Bayton

6.5

7.0 Neen Sollars

A456

7.8 Weir
Tetstill

8.2
Confluence

Newnham Bridge 10.0

A456

10.2
Weir

10.8
Confluence

A443

RIVER TEME

RIVER TEME

© MJH 1995

31

RIVER CLUN

The river Clun runs off the Black Mountain by the village of Anchor. It is a twisting river with a grade of 0/1. Overhanging and fallen trees will be the greatest hazard on this small river, It flows through a beautiful valley but may not be possible in dry conditions, it is best paddled just after rain or between October and March. Clun Y.H.A. hostel is 3 miles from Purlsow bridge.

N.R.A. RATING 1A   **O/S MAP No: 136**

MILES

0	Puslow bridge, (B4385), O.S. M/R 361 805, access down bank by side of bridge.
0.7	Clunbury bridges, two bridges.
2	River Kemp joins from the left, followed by a small island, small weir on the right side of the island shoot on the right.
2.1	Bridge.
2.3	Beambridge, bridge.
2.6	Bridge.
3.5	Railway bridge.
4	Weir, 600mm high shoot in centre.
5.2	Clungunford bridge, (B4367), access downstream left.
7.5	Broadway Hall bridge, (B4385).
9.8	Jay bridge.
10	River Redlake joins from the right.
10.8	Footbridge.
10.9	Lientwardine, confluence with the river Teme at 8.9 miles.
11	Lientwardine bridge, (B4113), small weir just after, egress onto common land downstream left.

RIVER ONNY

The river Onny begins as two streams, the West Onny which rises in Black Marsh to the West of the Village of Shelve & the East Onny which runs off Devils Chair to the East of Shelve in Shropshire. After joining at Eaton the Onny flows through Craven Arms & Onibury to join the river Teme near to Bromfield. The river flows through a narrow & twisting valley as far as Cheney Longville where the landscape becomes more flat & rural onward to Bromfield.

It is a quiet but interesting little river which needs rain to make it worthwhile, it has a grade of 0/1 but a major problem is going to be fallen trees & barbed wire strands.

N.R.A. RATING 1B   **O/S MAP No: 136**

MILES

0	Onibury bridge, (A49), access downstream left of the bridge. There may be a strand of barbed wire under the bridge.
0.8	Footbridge, farm on the right.
3.5	Bromfield bridge, (A49), egress on the right just after bridge onto public footpath. Parking by the church.
3.8	Confluence with the river Teme at 22.3 miles, Next egress at Linney Recreation ground in 2.3 miles.

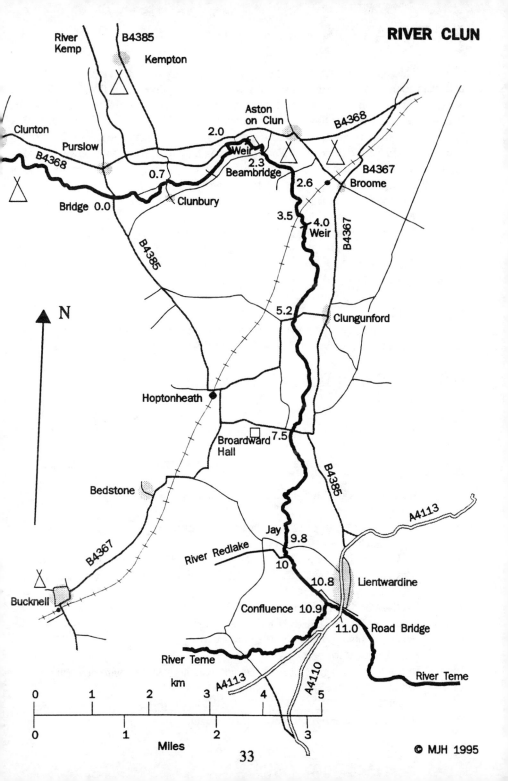

RIVER CLUN

© MJH 1995

33

RIVER AVON (WARWICKSHIRE)

The river Avon starts it's life on the Northamptonshire & Leicestershire border, it is than joined by a stream from Sulby Reservoir, the river then flow into Stanford Reservoir. After emerging from Rugby, Kenilworth, Warwick, Stratford, Evesham, Pershore & joins the river Severn at Tewkesbury.

The river is grade 0/1 through it's length with many weirs. At Stratford it becomes canalised for the rest of it's course, running still & deep with powered craft a hazard especially in the summer months. A feature of the navigable part are the locks & weirs all if which must be inspected & treated with caution in high water.

The river can be canoed from Rugby but may become clogged with weed in the summer months.

Permission must be sought to pass through sections before Stratford they are:-
Stoneleigh Park, the Estate Office, Stoneleigh Abbey, warks.
Warwick Castle Park, Park Office, Warwick, Warks.
Charlecote Park, The Curator, Charlecote Park, Warks.

MEMBERS ONLY

After Stratford Upon Avon there is a licence agreement covered by your B.C.U. membership. ALWAYS CARRY YOUR CARD.

N.R.A. RATING 1B TO 1.2 MILES, 2 AFTER

MILES   O/S MAP Nos: 140, 150/1

0	Rugby, Grand Union Canal aqueduct, portage from canal, shallows follow.
0.7	Avon Mill bridge, (A426).
1.2	Newbold on Avon bridge, access down bank by the bridge, good starting point.
1.7	Weir, shallows below, portage either side.
2	Railway bridge.
2.5	Island, go right, small weir at the end, portage right.
3.2	Little Lawford weir, shoot on the left.
3.3	Low footbridge, right arch best, NO HEADROOM IN FLOOD.
6.5	Kings Newnham Mill, (derelict), with footbridge, take left stream around mill.
6.7	Church Lawford bridge.
8.7	Bretford bridge, (A428).
9.2	Marston Mill, portage right into side stream.
10.5	Brandon railway & road bridge, beware low pipe.
13	Lake keep left for best exit.
14	Ryton Mill, portage left above the mill, watch for barbed wire downstream.
14.4	Ryton bridge, (A45).
17.5	Bubenhall Mill, PRIVATE WATER ABOVE THE MILL, land at the first weir and portage right to enter below the mill.

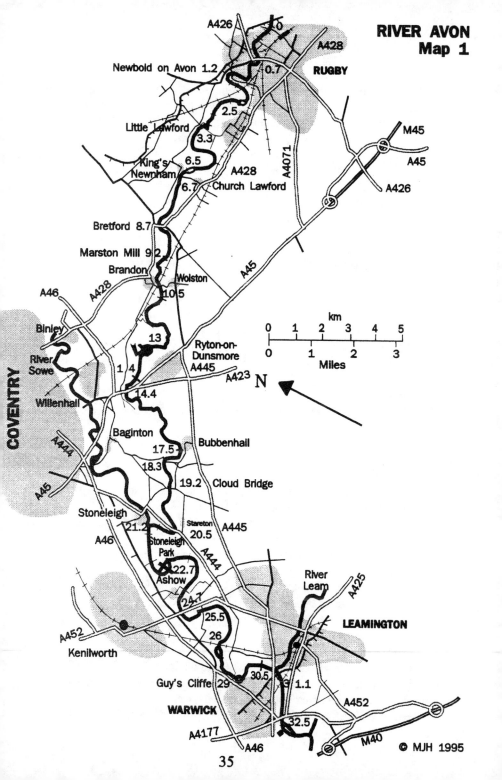

RIVER AVON
Map 1

35

18.3	Bubenhall bridge.
19.2	Cloud bridge, (A444), after this bridge the river enters Stoneleigh Park, there are several bridges in the park.
20.5	Stare bridge & coach bridge, left arch best.
21.2	River Sowe joins from the right, it is possible to canoe this tributary from Binley, a distance of 7 miles. Although it is a N.R.A. Grade 2 river in the last mile there is an outflow from a water treatment works which downgrades this river and the river Avon for some miles afterwards.
22.7	Stoneleigh Abbey, two weirs, the first can be portaged on the right, the second can be shot on the left. There are numerous bridge into the show ground here.
24.1	Ashow footbridge, the park ends here.
24.7	Chesford bridge, (A452).
25.5	Blackdown bridge.
26	Railway bridge.
29	Guys Cliff Mill, weir, can be portaged on the left.
29.7	Rock Mill weir, beware fallen masonry, portage right.
30.5	Portobello bridge, (A445), river Leam joins from the left.
31	Aqueduct, Grand Union canal, easy portage to the canal.
31.1	Railway bridge.
32.5	Warwick bridge, (A425), access from park upstream left, chain across bridge.
32.6	Warwick Castle, island, go right over weir or portage only left onto island.
35	Leafield bridge, (private road).
36	Bridge, (M40).
37	Barford Mill, disused, portage right between landing stages into lower stream.
37.5	Barford bridge, (A429), river shallow before the bridge.
42	Hampton Lucy Mill, land & portage right at the first weir before the mill, road bridge just after the mill.
42.5	Charlecote Park, there are deer gates at both sides of the park, the river Deane joins in the park, lots of rushes in the summer.
44.2	Alveston Mill, access from left bank by road, (B4086). Y.H.A. hostel.
46.2	Tiddington, access from end of lane at M/R 221 561.
48	Stratford bridges, (A3400/A422), Stratford canal joins from the right 100 metres a after the bridges.
48.5	Lucy's Mill weir, choice of two weirs, the right one has a stopper, left one is easier, portage on the left by the lock.
48.7	By-pass bridge, (A4300), & footbridge.
49	Weir Brake lock & weir.
49.8	Old railway bridge.
50	River Stour joins from the left, (see Stour guide).
51.5	Luddington, weir & lock, rocky in low water, shoot on the right in med/high water, land on concrete slipway to inspect, Regional slalom site.
53.2	Binton bridge, "Four Alls" public house upstream left, good lunch stop.

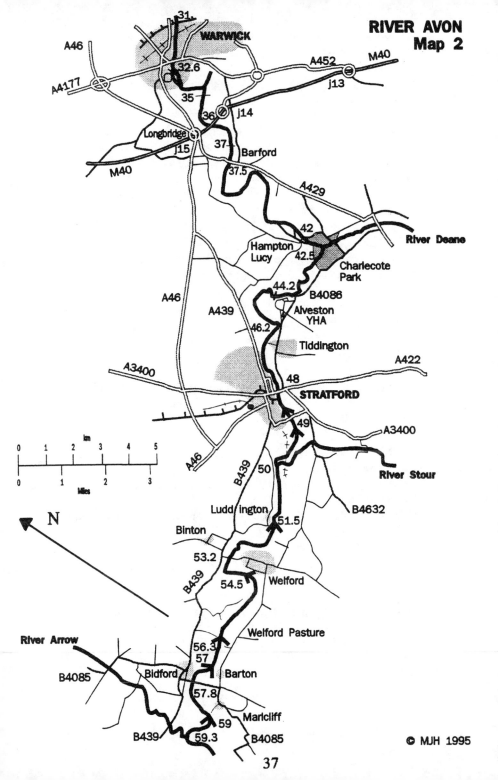

RIVER AVON
Map 2

31

WARWICK

A46

A452   M40

A4177   j13

32.6

35

36   j14

Longbridge

j15   37   Barford

M40

37.5   A429

42

Hampton
Lucy   42.5

Charlecote
Park   River Deane

A46   44.2

A439   B4086

Alveston
YHA

46.2

Tiddington

A3400   A422

48

STRATFORD

A46

49   A3400

B439   50   River Stour

Ludd ington   51.5   B4632

Binton

53.2

B439   54.5   Welford

Welford Pasture

River Arrow   56.3
57

B4085   Bidford   Barton

57.8

Marlcliff

59

B439   59.3   B4085

37

© MJH 1995

km
0   1   2   3   4   5

0   1   2   3
Miles

N

54.5	Welford lock & weir, weir gentle slope, easy in centre.
56.3	Pilgrim lock & weir.
57	Barton lock & weir.
57.8	Bideford bridge, (B4085), access from public park downstream left.
59	Marlcliff lock & weir.
59.3	River Arrow joins from the right, (see Arrow guide).
61.5	Harvington Mill, gently sloping weir left side of the river, shoot centre.
62	Fish & Anchor Inn, access from B4510 by the ford, alternative access by the caravan site 200 metres upstream, see site manager first.
62.2	Lock channel joins from the right, a good 1.8 mile novice circuit, over the weir, through the rapid, over the ford, up the lock channel, portage the lock , then back to the weir top.
64.5	Offenham, Evesham by-pass bridge, (A435).
65.1	Railway bridge.
65.4	Evesham lock & weir, shoot centre/right in low water, inspect in high water.
65.6	Evesham, Workman bridge, access from public park on the left after the bridge, good lunch stop, town on the right.
66.1	Evesham bridge, access from public park upstream right, large car park.
66.4	River Isbourne joins from the left.
66.9	Hampton Ferry, wire across river.
67.5	Railway bridge.
68.5	Chadbury lock & weir, shoot on the right.
70.5	Railway bridge, Fladbury Canoe Club boathouse on the right just after.
71	Fladbury lock & weir, shoot anywhere, access upstream right bank by weir top, parking 100 metres.
71.2	Fladbury bridge, (Jubilee bridge).
75.5	Wyre Mill lock & weir, shoot on the left.
76.5	Pershore lock & weir.
77	Pershore bridges, old then new, (A44), access from car park between bridges.
81.7	Nafford lock & weir.
83.5	Eckington bridge, (B4080), access from car park upstream left bank.
84	Railway bridge.
85.5	Strensham lock & weir.
85.6	Footbridge.
88	Motor way bridge, (M5).
91	Tewkesbury lock & weir, weir on the right must be portaged, river Severn is now 800 metres down this branch. Alternatively carry straight on down the town branch to reach the river Severn in approximately 1 mile.
91.5	Confluence with the river Severn at 164.1 miles.

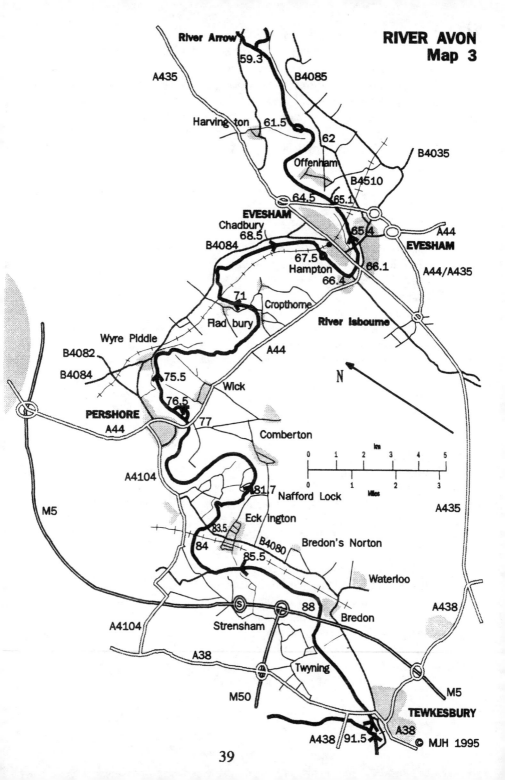

RIVER AVON
Map 3

River Arrow

A435

59.3

B4085

Harvington   61.5

62

B4035

Offenham

B4510

64.5   65.1

EVESHAM

Chadbury   65.4

68.5   EVESHAM

B4084

A44

67.5   66.1

Hampton   A44/A435

66.4

71

Cropthorne

Flad bury   River Isbourne

Wyre Piddle

B4082   A44

B4084   75.5

Wick   N

76.5

PERSHORE   77

A44   Comberton

A4104   km
0   1   2   3   4   5

81.7 Nafford Lock
Eckington   0   1   2   3
Miles

A435

83.5

M5   84   B4080   Bredon's Norton

85.5

Waterloo

A438

88

Strensham   Bredon

A4104

A38

Twyning

M5

M50

TEWKESBURY

A438   91.5   A38   © MJH 1995

39

RIVER STOUR (Warwickshire)

The river Stour rises at Stour Well in Oxfordshire, after which it flows through Shipstone to join the river Avon just after Stratford-on-Avon. The river is narrow so there will be a possibility of tree and rubbish jams which may require portaging. Permission to pass through Alscot Park has been refused in the past & the portage around the park will require a vehicle so this may spoil the tour. The section from Shipstone to Halford is an ideal tour for spring or Autumn but may require some rain. The last 1.6 miles from Clifford Mill by the A46 bridge can be an ideal lead into the river Avon.

N.R.A. RATING 1B   O/S MAP No: 151

MILES

0	Shipstone on Stour bridge, (B4035), access from downstream banks.
0.8	River divides, go left over weir, straight drop.
1	Fell Mill bridge.
1.6	Bridge.
2.2	Honington Hall weir, shoot centre, straight drop.
2.4	Weir, at the end of a wood. the river runs quite fast as it skirts Tredington, slows down & meanders to Halford.
5.4	Halford bridge, (A429), weir, then new road bridge followed by the old bridge, easy access & parking.
6.6	Weir.
7.6	Bridge.
7.9	Bridge, (A3400), and weir.
8	Bridge and weir.
9.2	Bridge.
11.2	Wimpstone bridge.
11.6	Bridge.
12.1	Preston on Stour bridge, the river divides just before the bridge, the right stream goes immediately over a weir, weir in 200 metres on the left stream.
12.2	River joins again. (Alscot Park from 12.1 to 12.7 miles).
12.6	Weir, river divides.
12.7	Bridges, one on each stream, river joins in 100metres.
13.4	River divides, go over weir on right stream.
13.5	Bridge & weir, river joins in 200metres.
13.8	River divides, go down left stream.
13.9	Bridge, access downstream left, road, (B4632), left.
14	River joins then flows under bridge, (B4632).
15.3	Old railway bridge.
15.5	Confluence with the river Avon at 50 miles.

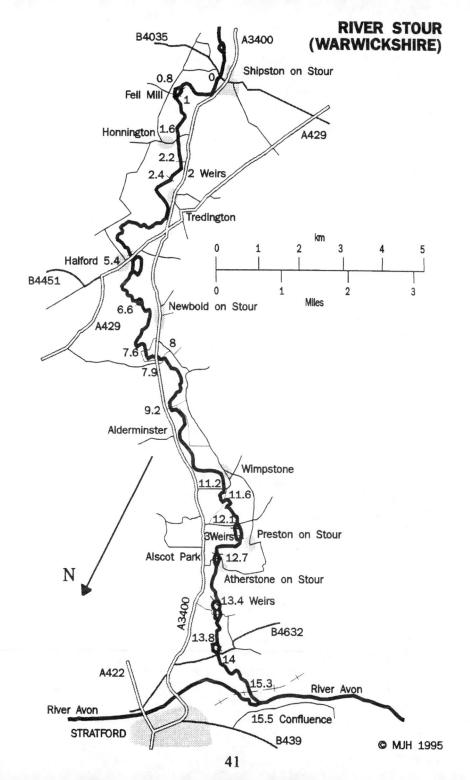

RIVER STOUR
(WARWICKSHIRE)

41

RIVER LEAM

The river Leam rises by Hellidon in Northamptonshire, from here it flows in a Westerly direction through Marton & Leamington to join the river Avon close to the town. It is only a stream for the first 10 miles of it's course & only when it joins with Rawlings Brook does it become canoeable. It is possible from this point in spate but the general starting point is Marton.

It is a narrow rural river with farmland forming it's banks & has a grade of 0/1.

Permission must be sought to pass through two sections, they are:-

H Johnson, Offchurch bury, Leamington Spa, Warks.

E Willes, Newbold Comlyn, Leamington Spa, Warks.

N.R.A. RATING 2   O/S MAP No: 151/2

MILES

0	Marton bridge, (A423), there may not be enough water here during the summer.
	Access upstream right over style, car park 3 cars. Short walk to Itchen confluence.
0.1	River Itchen joins from the left, water level improves.
1	Stoneyford bridge.
1.7	Eathorpe bridge & weir.
3.8	Hunnington bridge.
5.2	Ford, shallows.
6.5	Offchurch bridge.
7.8	Ford Farm bridge.
8.5	Offchurch Bury Mill & weirs. As the river approaches the mill three weirs flow off to the right. THREE ROUTES,
	BEST ROUTE, weir (1), can be shot on the right.
8.7	Weirs 2/3, shoot on the right but has obstructions at the foot, always inspect. PORTAGE RIGHT, DO NOT PORTAGE LEFT.
9	River runs close to the Grand Union canal.
10.5	Access point, large car park.
11	Willes bridge, river enters a park and widens into a boating lake.
11.2	Footbridge & weir, the weir is just after the bridge, there is a chain across the top. The depth of water at the foot is uncertain, may be O.K. in a plastic boat.
11.4	Victoria bridge, (A452), end of the park, NO EGRESS.
11.8	Leamington Spa Canoe Club boathouse on the right, road access through the college.
12	Princess Drive, railway & road bridges.
12.1	Weir, usually dry along most of it's length, but 2 metres gap on the left has wooden boards to control water level, again will be O.K. in a plastic boat.
12.5	Confluence with the river Avon at 30.5 miles. Next egress in half a mile into Grand Union canal at bridge.

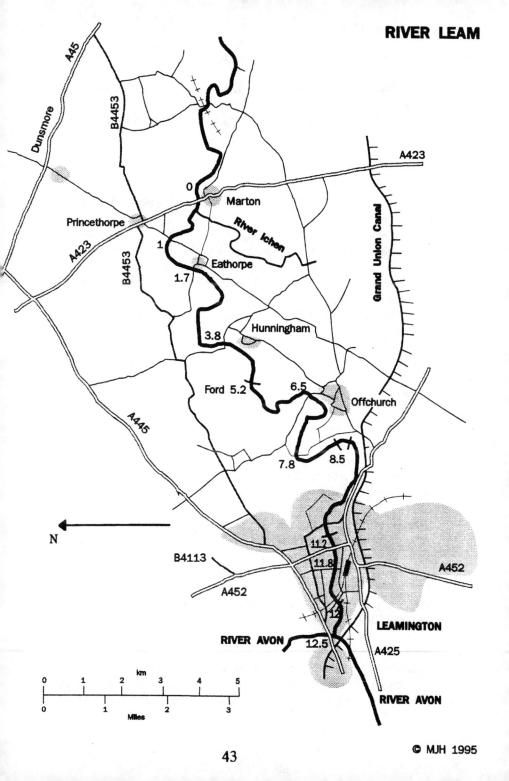

RIVER LEAM

© MJH 1995

RIVER ARROW (Warwickshire)

The river Arrow runs off the East side if the Lickey Hills & becomes catchmented
into the two Bittell reservoirs. From here it flows South to Alvechurh, Redditch, Alcester & goes on to join the river Avon at Salford Priors.

It is a small river so the water level will be linked with the weather & so it is best canoed after rain. Grade 0/1.

N.R.A. RATING 2   O/S MAP No: 150

MILES

0	Spernall bridge, start for high water, shallow until the island. Access by bridge, Limited parking.
0.2	Footbridge.
2	Ford & footbridge, watch for rocks under the bridge, island in 100 metres, go left for the main stream, this ends in a small shoot, good play spot. Weir on the right side will be dry except in high water. Access from ford turn off A435 S/P Coughton Fields.
2.2	Bridge followed by a ford in 100 metres.
2.4	Footbridge.
3.2	Weir, 600mm high.
3.5	Weir, large tow back in high water.
3.7	Weir.
4	Road bridge, (B4089).
4.6	Bridge.
4.7	River divides, go left.
4.8	River Alne joins from the left. Access for low water, park in old roadway & get in by the bridge, see Alne guide.
4.9	Footbridge, old A46/A422 road bridge.
5.2	Small weir, good play wave.
5.4	Small weir.
5.9	Bridge (A46).
6.2	Arrow Mill weir, shoot sharp left or right, inspect in high water, double drop, 1st large drop, large stopper, 2nd small drop, large stopper. Bank support essential.
6.7	Footbridge.
7.6	Wixford bridge, (B4085), small weir, beware tow back, egress into pub car park ask landlord first.
8.3	Broom Mill weir.
8.4	Broom Mill bridge.
10.4	Salford bridge, (A439), last egress before the river Avon.
11	Confluence with the river Avon at 59.5 miles, next egress on the river Avon, downstream half a mile to Cleeve Prior or upstream half a mile to Marcliff.

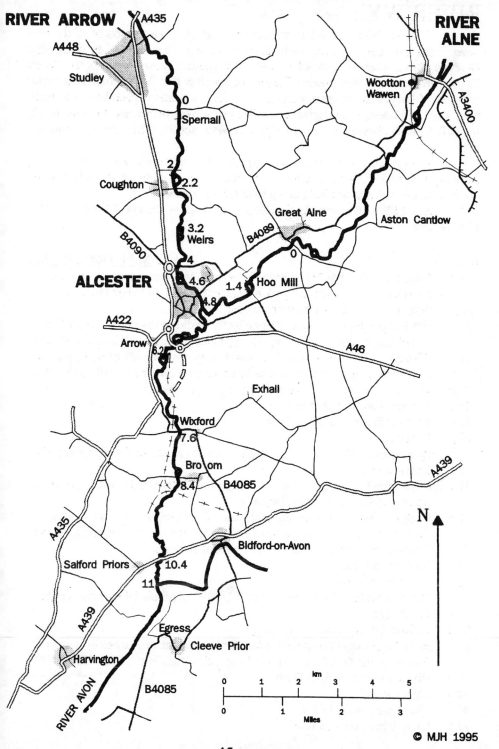

RIVER ARROW

RIVER ALNE

A435

A448

Studley

Wootton Wawen

A3400

0
Spernall

2
Coughton 2.2

Great Alne

Aston Cantlow

3.2
Weirs

B4089

0

4

ALCESTER

4.6

1.4 Hoo Mill

4.8

A422

A46

Arrow

6.2

Exhall

Wixford

7.6

Broom

A439

8.4 B4085

Bidford-on-Avon

Salford Priors 10.4

11

A435

A439

Egress

Cleeve Prior

Harvington

RIVER AVON

B4085

km
0   1   2   3   4   5

0   1   2   3
Miles

N

© MJH 1995

B4090

45

RIVER WYE

The river Wye runs off Plynlimon Fawr not far from the source of the river Severn. The river flows in a Southerly direction through Rhayader, Builth Wells, Hay, Hereford, Ross, Monmouth & Chepstow, after which it flows out into the Severn Estuary near to the Severn bridge. The part of the river that flows through the region runs from Glasbury to the estuary and is an ancient navigation which has come under the control of a management system controlled by the Wye Management Group lead by the N.R.A. It is advisable to contact the river Wye Access Officer before planning a tour.

The section within the region is grade 0/1 in average water, there are many small rapids to make a tour enjoyable in low water, many of these are washed out as the water rises, this makes it an ideal touring river for the summer.

ACCESS: C Charters, Eagle Hotel, New Radnor, Powys. LD8 4SN. TEL: 0154421 208

MILES	O/S MAP Nos: 149, 162

48.4	Glasbury bridge, (A438), shallows after, keep left, access through gate by scout hut upstream left, car park by public toilets, Wye Valley canoe shop.
52.4	Wyecliffe Weir, more a rock/shingle bank.
53.9	Hay bridge, (B4351), rocky section by the bridge in low water, access from outfall "steps" onto public footpath, right bank. Camping, TEL: 0497 847371
58.4	Whitney Toll Bridge, (B4350), access slipway upstream left bank, £1 per boat is charged for it's use, it is possible to negotiate a party rate. TEL: 0432 669
59.2	The Boat Inn, left bank, access by prior permission only.
63.6	Turners Boat, go left of island.
66.9	Bredwardine bridge, access forbidden here.
69.9	Bridge ruins.
71	Bycross campsite, land on right bank 50 metres above the falls ask permission from nearby farm.
71.1	Monnington Falls, left channel goes over a rock ledge but this will be dry in low water, shallow on the right channel.
71.3	Campsite, land by fishing hut, right bank, where telephone wires cross the river. Permission from Mr & Mrs Priest, at farmhouse 200 metre form church.
72.9	Bridge Sollers, bridge, access from upstream left bank.
78.9	Lower Eaton Island.
81.8	Old railway bridge.
82.4	Hereford bridges, (A49), new, then old, access from park downstream right .
82.9	Footbridge.
83.4	Railway bridge, rapids under bridge.
88.9	River Lugg joins from the left, Mordiford bridge can be reached by going up the river Lugg for 800 metres, see Lugg guide. Camping, TEL: 0432 8702213
89.4	Holme Lacey bridge, (B4399).
90.9	Cherry Island
96.3	Site of old railway bridge.
97.5	Carey Island, go right side.

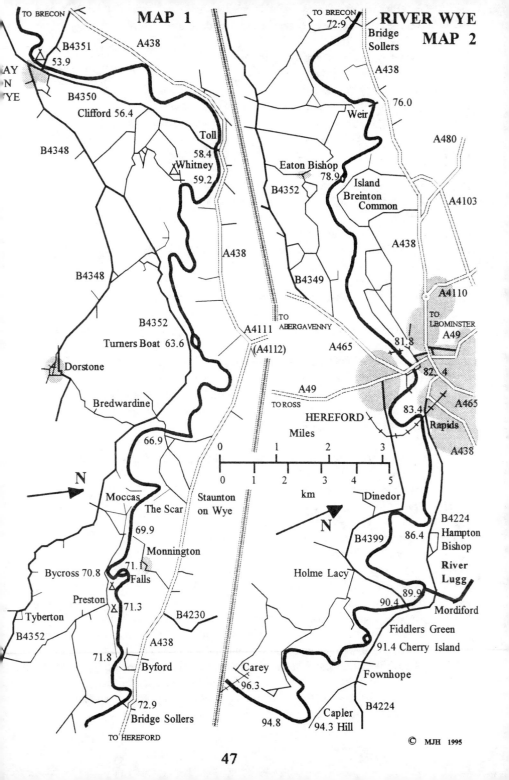

97.9	Wooded islands, three channels have rapids in low water.
99.9	Hoarwithy bridge.
101.2	Sellack bridge, suspension footbridge.
102.5	Site of railway bridge, pillars in river.
106.7	Stream joins from the right.
107.7	Hole in the Wall, section of small rapids and islands.
108.2	Foy bridge, suspension footbridge, access downstream left into lay-by.
110.2	Site of railway bridge.
110.7	Bridge, (A40, A449), campsite downstream right.
111.2	Ross on Wye.
111.7	Wilton bridge, island and shallows below bridge.
115.7	Kern bridge, (B4234), inns on left bank. Access ramp. Site of old railway bridge.
118.2	Lydbrook, rapid in low water.
118.7	Welsh Bicknor Y.H.A. hostel by church on the right.
119	Bicknor railway bridge.
122.4	Huntsham bridge.
124.4	Symonds yat, rapid down left bank, break out pools on the right side. Rapid is used for recreational paddling and for slaloms. Camping, TEL: 01600 890129
125.7	Trestle and rope bridge, **PLEASE KEEP LEFT FROM NOW ON**.
130.2	Monmouth bridge, (A466), two access sites on both banks, advance permission **MUST** be gained from the following addresses:- The secretary, Monmouth Rowing Club, Wyeside, Old Dixon Road, Master in charge of canoeing, Monmouth Sclhool, Monmouth, Gwent. NP5 3XP. Please note, no fires, take all your litter with you.
130.7	River Monnow joins from the right, confused rapids below. The river Monnow has been canoed from Pandy (30 miles), in med/high water, it is mostly grade 1 but has occasional parts with grade 2,3 or even 4 in spate. Camping & Y.H.A. hostel.
130.8	Two old railway bridges.
131.2	River Trothy joins from the right.
132.9	Redbrook railway bridge.
136.2	Bigsweir bridge, (A466), approximate limit of tide.
136.7	Bigsweir, rapid to the right of island, between here and Chepstow there are many ground weirs which are covered at high tide, not difficult but care may be necessary. St Briavels Y.H.A. hostel 2 miles.
139.7	Brockweir bridge.
141	Tintern, weir & bridge, last landing before Chepstow, land on ferry slipway. Best time to run this last section is on the high tide, 1hour before the tide turns at Tintern, there may be a 30ft rise and fall on the tide.
148.2	Chepstow bridge, egress at steps downstream right of the bridge, mud bank at low tide.High tide is Dover minus 4 hours. Don't go any further unless you are equipped for the sea, the Bristol Channel has strong currents and tides and therefore must be treated with respect.

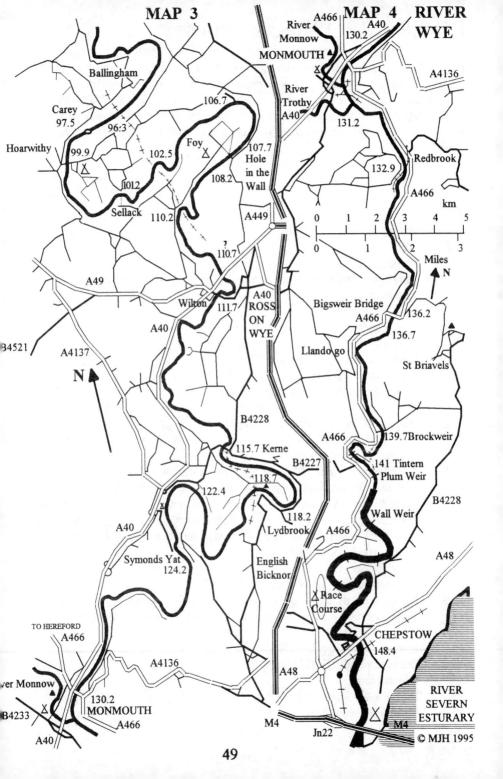

RIVER ARROW (HEREFORDSHIRE)

The river Arrow runs off the East side of Gwaun-Ceste-Hill near New Radnor. It flows in an Easterly direction through Kington & Eardisland to join the river Lugg just after Leominster. Although it is 25 miles long only 17 are Canoeable & then only in wet weather, the river is not practical in low water but is ideal in med/high water. The river's course takes it through some lovely pastoral countryside which makes it an unexciting river which is punctuated by many weirs which are generally safe & in good condition.

N.R.A. RATING 2   O/S MAP No: 137

MILES

0	Hunton bridge.
0.5	Weir
1.3	Forge Mill ford.
1.5	Old railway bridge, there are 3 weirs in the next 2 miles inspect first.
3.5	Saunton Mill.
4	Bridge.
4.5	River divides.
5	Bridge.
5.1	Leen Farm, river joins again.
5.2	Old railway bridge.
6	Pembridge bridge, access from upstream bank.
8	Folly Farm weir, just after a left hand bend, shoot on the right side.
8.4	Bridge, access from downstream right bank.
8.6	Eardisland bridge, this village has won awards & is very pretty & interesting, well worth a stop & look.
8.8	Eardisland Mill weir, **IMPORTANT**, shoot over weir at a quarter of it's width from the right hand end or portage down sluice. Mill race is private property.
10.1	River divides, two routes, **RIGHT ROUTE**, weir 500cm high, the route after this winding and narrow, watch for barbed wire. **LEFT ROUTE**, tight right bend in 100 metres, the Arrow Mill weir, 1 metre high, best shot left end.
10.3	Arrow Green bridge, (A4110).
12.7	River divides.
12.9	Monkland bridge, (A44).
13.9	Irvington Court, large pool on left hand bend overlooked by the house. Tippetts Brook joins from right into the pool, bridge over the river at exit.
14.4	Irvington bridge.
15.6	Bridge.
16.1	Broadway bridge, (B4326).
16.7	Railway bridge.
16.8	Bridge, (A49), Leominster by-pass, no egress here.
17.2	Confluence with the river Lugg at 19.9 miles.

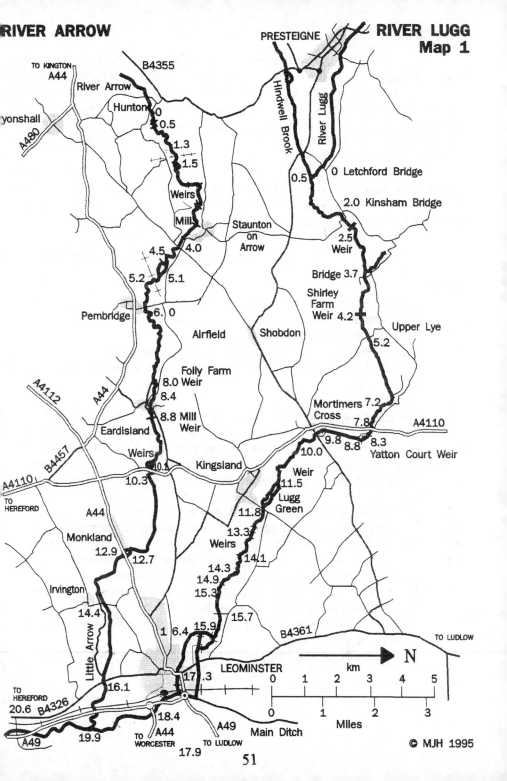

RIVER ARROW

RIVER LUGG
Map 1

TO KINGTON
A44
B4355
River Arrow
Hunton 0
0.5
1.3
1.5
Weirs
Mill
4.5 4.0
5.2 5.1
Pembridge 6.0
Airfield
Folly Farm
8.0 Weir
8.4
8.8 Mill
Weir
Eardisland
Weirs
10.1
10.3
Kingsland
A44
Monkland
12.9 12.7
Irvington
14.4
16.4
15.9
16.1
18.4
20.6 B4326
19.9
17.9
TO WORCESTER
A44
A49
TO LUDLOW
Main Ditch
LEOMINSTER
17.3
B4361
TO LUDLOW
N
Little Arrow

yonshall
A480
A4112
A44
B4457
A4110
TO HEREFORD
A4110
TO HEREFORD
A49

PRESTEIGNE
Hindwell Brook
River Lugg
0.5
0 Letchford Bridge
2.0 Kinsham Bridge
2.5 Weir
Bridge 3.7
Shirley Farm
Weir 4.2
Upper Lye
5.2
Mortimers 7.2
Cross 7.8
9.8 8.8 8.3
10.0 Yatton Court Weir
A4110
Weir
11.5
Lugg Green
11.8
13.3 Weirs
14.1
14.3
14.9
15.3
15.7

Staunton on Arrow
Shobdon

km
0 1 2 3 4 5

0   1   2   3
Miles

© MJH 1995

51

RIVER LUGG

The river Lugg has it's source on Beacon Hill near to the village of Crug in Powys. It then flows in a South-westerly direction through Presteigne, Leominster, Hereford to join the river Wye near to Mordiford. The river flows through a wooded landscape in it's upper reaches & farmland forms the most parts of it's banks as it slowly meanders along towards the river Wye. It is unusual as it changes it's name as it flows into Leominster with the river Lugg skirting the town and Kenwater flowing through, Kenwater being the main stream and the Lugg a drainage ditch.

The usual starting place is Letchmore bridge. The upper part of the river can be shallow in the summer, it is best canoed between October & March. A feature of the upper section is it's many weirs & bends with wave "cushions" on trees & banks, not a river for the raw novice. An ideal river for improvers and for proficiency testing.

<u>O/S MAP Nos: 129, 142</u>

MILES

0	Letchmoor bridge, access, turn right off B4362 just past Combe going West, into unclassified road S/P Kinsham, bridge in half a mile.
0.5	Hindwell Brook joins from the right.
2	Kinsham bridge, access from field upstream left, (farmer friendly).
2.5	Weir, N.R.A. gauging weir, shallow "V" good play wave shoot centre all states.
3.7	Bridge.
4.2	Shirley farm weir, there is a rocky fall straight ahead, if you take the right channel you will come to the weir in 200 metres. The weir is not a practical proposition as it has a rocky flow breaker at the foot. BEST ROUTE: over the rocky fall & down the small stream to join the main river just below the weir.
5.2	Upper Lye bridge, access, upstream left bank, car park, ideal for emergency car.
7.2	The Leathers weir, shoot far end in high water. Portage right end.
7.8	Aymestry bridge, (A4110), egress upstream right into pub car park.
8.3	Yatton Court weir No:1, on a left hand bend, 1 metre drop over a gentle slope.
8.8	Yatton Court weir No:2, easy slope, small drop at the bottom into a pool, Large but generally safe wave in high water, difficult portage.
9.8	Mortimers Cross mill weir, 1.5 metres drop over an easy slope, shoot centre. Always inspect in high water, large tow back.
10	Mortimers Cross bridge, (B4362), access downstream right bank. Park in lay-by 100 metres to the West.
10.8	Island, left side not possible in low water, go right may be blocked by trees.

11.5	Lugg Green weir, easy slope.
11.8	Kingsland bridge.
	THE NEXT THREE NEW WEIRS MUST BE CAREFULLY INSPECTED.
12.9	Weir, do not attempt central fish ladder, it is a series of boxes which will catch canoe nose. Shoot either side in low water only, portage in high water.
13.3	Weir, much larger than first weir and so is not advisable even in low water.
13.6	Weir, same design as previous two weirs but is smaller, shoot sides with support.
14.1	Weir, Victorian, easy slope.
14.3	Weir, easy slope.
14.9	Weir, inspect in high water.
15.3	Weir, inspect in high water, river Lugg leaves to the left, not practical. Kenwater carries on as the main stream.
15.7	Bridge.
15.8	Egress point, lane comes close to the left bank, carry across field.
15.9	Weirs, these are two new weirs side by side, the left weir carries water into the "Main Ditch" a flood protection culvert which joins the river Lugg in half a mile. This weir is very narrow with a fierce tow back, do not attempt. The main weir is unshootable due to anti-scour teeth at the foot. Portage right bank.
16.4	Farm bridge.
16.9	Stream joins from the right.
17	Small weir.
17.3	Leominster bridge, (A44).
17.4	Access point, up slipway into public car park.
17.5	Footbridge, cast iron, (Worcester Foundry 1844).
17.6	Railway bridge.
17.7	River Lugg joins from the left.
17.8	Bridge near to Leominster station, small rapid. Access across railway footbridge into industrial estate.
18	Bridge, (A49). No egress.
18.4	Eaton bridge, (A44),
18.8	Bridge and weir, inspect first, portage right.
19.3	Bridge.
19.9	River Arrow joins from the right, (see Arrow guide).
20.6	Ford bridge.
22	Hampton bridge, (A417).
22.3	Bridge.
23.5	Hampton Court weir and bridge, weir unshootable, portage left.
24.5	Bodenham bridge.
24.9	Bodenahm Church footbridge.

26.5	Dinmore railway bridge, small rapid under.
28.5	Railway bridge.
30	Walkers Green bridge.
31.6	Moreton bridge, egress downstream right, parking not good.
33.2	Wergins bridge.
34.2	Wergins Stone, old stone canal aqueduct, take the left channel.
35	Railway bridge.
36	Bridge, (A4103).
37.5	Lugwardine bridge, (A438), access not practical here.
38.1	Weir.
39.5	River Frome joins from the left.
41	Mordiford bridge, (B4224), inspect before shooting mill channel.
41.5	Confluence with the river Wye at 88.9 miles.

RIVER ALNE

The river Alne runs off Gorcott Hill & flows through Henley in Arden, Wooton Wawen, Great Alne to join the river Arrow at Alcester. It is a small rural river which depends on some rainfall before it becomes canoeable. The river has a grade of 0/1 & can be an interesting lead into the Arrow.

N.R.A. RATING 1B   O/S MAP No: 150

MILES

0	Great Alne bridge.
1.4	Hoo Mill weir, go right at island for main stream, there are two weirs in 100 metres, always inspect first.
3.4	Confluence with the river Arrow at 4.8 miles, see Arrow guide for access.

SEE ARROW MAP PAGE 45

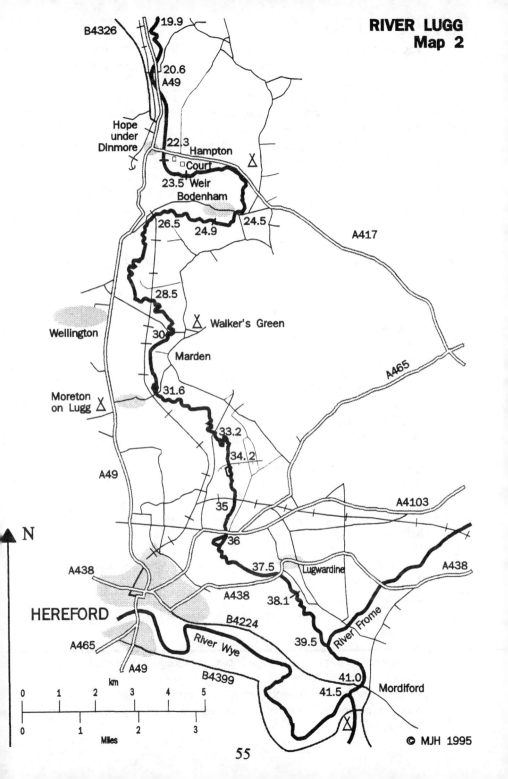

RIVER LUGG
Map 2

B4326

19.9

20.6
A49

Hope
under
Dinmore

22.3
Hampton
Court

23.5 Weir
Bodenham

26.5   24.9   24.5

A417

28.5

Walker's Green

Wellington

30

Marden

Moreton
on Lugg

31.6

A465

33.2

34.2

A49

35

A4103

N

36

37.5   Lugwardine   A438

A438

38.1

A438

HEREFORD

B4224

River Frome

39.5

A465

River Wye

A49

B4399

41.0   Mordiford

41.5

km

0   1   2   3   4   5

0   1   2   3
Miles

© MJH 1995

55

RIVER TRENT

The river Trent rises on Biddulph Moor & flows South through Stoke-on-Trent, after this it turns to the East and flows through Stone, Rugeley, Alrewas, Burton and onwards North until it joins the river Ouse by Goole.

It is a rural and unexciting river which has a grade of 0/1 for it's entire length. It is a public navigation . Pollution has been a great problem in the past, but the river is getting cleaner as the years go by as conservation measures are taking effect.

The river only becomes canoeable after Stoke-on-Trent as it is contained in low tunnels under the city. The best start is Trentham.

The section covered by this guide is the most interesting for canoeists as the river becomes canalised after Shardlow. For most of it's route the river is shadowed by the Trent and Mersey Canal, this makes a large number of circular tours possible, (see Trent Circles).

N.R.A. RATING 2   O/S MAP Nos: 118, 127/8

MILES

0	Trentham bridge, (B5035), the river enters Trentham gardens, there are 5 bridges in the park, the last followed by a 500cm high weir.
1.5	Strongford bridge, (A34).
2.7	Barlaston bridge.
5.7	Darlaston bridge, (A34).
7	Stone by-pass bridge, (A34).
7.2	Railway bridge.
7.3	Canal very close to left bank.
7.7	Walton bridge, Stafford and Stone Canoe Club slalom site and clubhouse downstream left.
9.4	Bridge, (A51), canal close by.
9.5	Aston footbridge.
11	Footbridge.
13.2	Sandon bridge, (B5066).
14.5	Salt bridge, village on the right.
15.2	Weir.
16	Gayton Brook, joins from the left, followed by an old railway bridge then road bridge (A518).
17.3	Bridge.
18.2	Bridge, weir underneath, inspect first, portage left.
19.2	Hoomill bridge.
20	Haywood Mill bridge, followed by the aqueduct of the Staffs and Worcestershire canal, **LOW HEADROOM**, portage left to canal.
20.5	Great Haywood, the river flows over a 30cm high weir, river Sow joins at the foot of the weir. Old stone footbridge in 20 metres. Access left bank between weir and footbridge. Village 300 metres left up footpath, parking , shops.
21.7	Railway bridge.

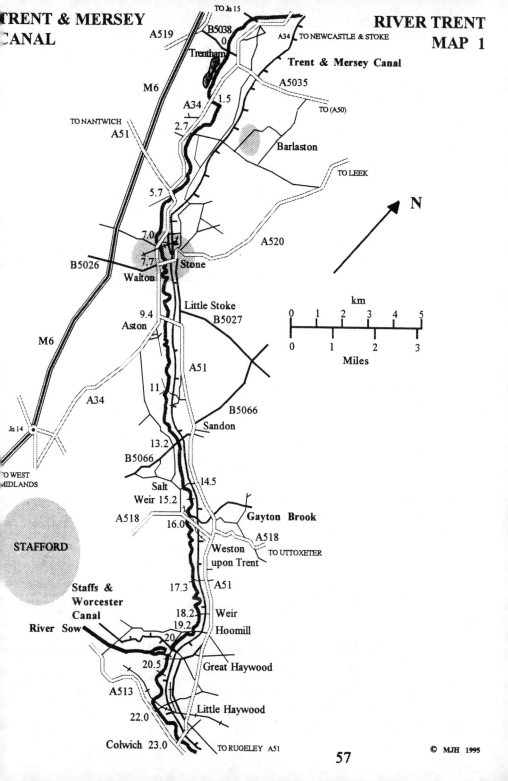

22	Seven Springs Bridge.
23	Colwich bridge (A51).
25.5	Canal aqueduct, **LOW HEADROOM**, portage to canal possible.
26.5	Rugeley bridge, (B5013).
27	Railway bridge.
28.5	Railway bridge.
29	Mavesyn Ridware footbridge, for access see Trent Circles.
29.8	High Bridges, (B5014), island after, best go left side, access between bridges.
30.5	Pipe bridge.
31	Nethertown footbridge.
31.5	Nethertown Island, two routes,

RIGHT ROUTE: main mill weir in 600 metres usually dry, best route over small weir in 400 metres into small stream which emerges at foot of main weir, bridge in 300 metres, watch for barbed wire. Access right in 200 metres by gate into lay-by on A515 after Kings Bromley going North.

LEFT ROUTE: go over small broken weir, in 600 metres the river Blithe joins from the left, after a further 400 metres egress right onto island just after a small stream, portage across the island to a point opposite the gate, cross left route stream to gate into lay-by as above.

33	Yoxall bridge, (A515), no access.
37	Alrewas Mill on right.
37.2	Metal bridge.
37.4	Metal footbridge, this carries the towpath of the Trent & Mersey canal across the river, lock gate on the right.
37.5	Canal leaves to the left, duck under chevrons on wire to keep on the main river, weir in 20 metres, safe in all but spate, portage right. Access get out by lock on the left, portage round lock paddle up canal to first bridge in village.
38.2	Wychnor bridge, (A38), no access A38 is a clearway. Campsite by prior arrangement, downstream right bank best egress inside of next right hand bend. Camping contact, Willowbrook farm 0283 790217 (G/R 183157).
38.5	Island, Swinfen K.C. slalom site, left channel clear, right channel for slalom. Access: club secretary address in year book.
39	Railway bridge.
39.2	River Tame joins from the right, (see Tame guide), this river has been grossly polluted in the past, it has improved a lot but still spoils the river Trent.
39.3	River Mease joins from the right.
39.9	Cotton Hall island, right side best.
43	Walton-on-Trent, bridge, access downstream right bank. Small car park.
46.7	Railway bridge.
47.3	Footbridge, pedestrian access left bank, Boathouse Inn right bank, canoeists welcome.
47.4	Burton-on-Trent, St Peters bridge, (A5121), just after the bridge a side channel leaves to the left, this channel goes through a public park and comes very close to the town, it emerges near to the top of Abbey weir.
47.8	River divides, **TWO ROUTES**

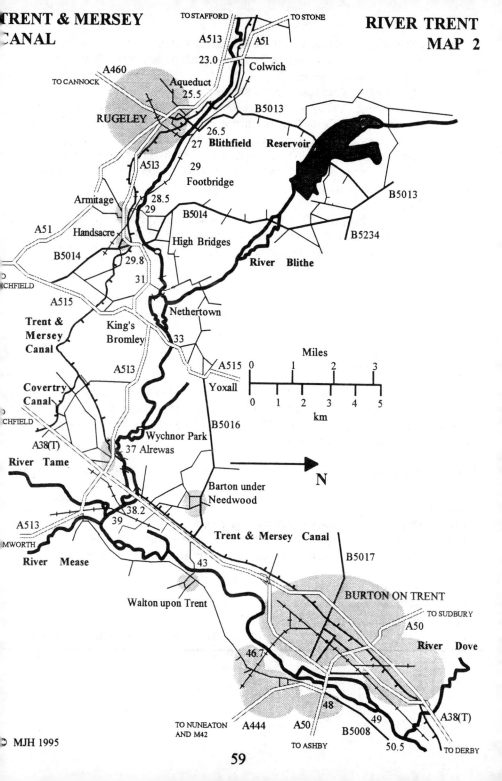

LEFT ROUTE, through route, in 300 metres there is Abbey weir, a slightly curved weir at an angle across the river just before the bridge. Shoot centre. Footbridge in 300 metres.

RIGHT ROUTE, camping and visiting Burton Canoe Clubhouse,

48.1   Abbey bridge (A50), just before the bridge on the right is the Rowing club and sea cadet centre, Canoe Club boathouse 400 mts downstream right of bridge. good access, car parking and camping next to the club house. Access/camping, advance permission MUST be sought (0283 33416). In a further 800 metres, weir, usually too dry in low water and has a bad stopper in spate. Left route is best through route.

49   River joins up again.

50.5   Newton Solney, river Dove joins from the left. Access from common land by Trent lane, Newton Solney. This is also the border with Derbyshire, the river Trent now leaves the region. Next egress is at Twyford Ferry, G.R. 327 284.

~~~~~~~~~~~~~~~~~~~~~~~~~~~~~~~~~~~~~

RIVER SOW

The river Sow rises in Bishops Wood to the east of Market Drayton. Its little more than a stream until it joins with the river Penk. It is grade 0/1 in most states. Because the river will generally be paddled as part of a Penk tour the mileage has been carried on from that of the river Penk.

N.R.A. RATING 2   O/S MAP No: 127

MILES

18.4   Queensville, confluence with the river Penk.

18.9   St Thomas's Priory bridge, access through gate downstream right.

20.9   Canal aqueduct, Staffs & Worcs canal, LOW HEADROOM IN HIGH WATER
portage possible to canal.

21.1   Milford bridge.

22.2   Shrugborough park bridge, (site of).

23   Great Haywood, river Trent joins from the left over a small weir. Egress onto grass bank between weir and stone footbridge.

SEE MAP ON PAGE 67

TRENT VALLEY CIRCLES

The valley of the river Trent offers some unique opportunities for circular tours. The river is followed by the Trent & Mersey Canal which comes close by in a number of places.

TOUR 1

Alrewas to Armitage and return (approx. 15 miles)

CANAL

MILES

0	New bridge, (A513), just by Bagnall Lock No: 13.
0.75	Common Lock.
1.3	Hunts Lock.
1.35	Bridge No: 50.
1.4	Keepers Lock.
1.5	Junction bridge.
1.55	Junction Lock.
1.65	Fradley Junction, the Coventry Canal joins from the left , pub food.
1.75	Middle Lock.
1.85	Shade House Lock and bridge.
2.1	Woodend Lock and bridge.
3.2	Bridge, (A515).
3.6	Bridge 55.
4.6	Tuppenhurst bridge.
4.8	Bridge 57.
5.2	Handsacre bridge, (A513), pub, shop, fish & chip shop.
5.55	Bridge 59.
5.75	Railway bridge.
6.05	Bridge 60, egress point in 100 metres on the right, footpath goes down a tunnel under the railway to emerge on the footbridge.

RIVER TRENT

6.05	Mavesyn Ridware footbridge, access downstream left from shingle bank.
6.9	High Bridges, (A513), go left of island after.
7.6	Pipe bridge.
8.1	Nethertown footbridge.
8.6	Nethertown Island, two routes, best route go left over small broken weir, this is the main stream, right route can be blocked by debris & the weir is usually dry.
10	Yoxall bridge,(A515), no egress here.
14	Metal (Bailey) bridge.
14.1	Metal footbridge, this carries the towpath of the Trent & Mersey canal across the river, lock gate is on the right, turn right into canal.
14.9	Start point, (A513), bridge.

TOURS 2/3

Long tour (16.4 miles), Great Haywood to Armitage & return. Short tour (9.5 miles), Great Haywood to Rugeley & return.

RIVER

MILES

0	Great Haywood, access from lane. Left off A51 going North through the centre of the village (S/P public footpath, Shugborough Hall). Lane goes under railway then crosses the canal then narrows to a footbridge over the river. Launch from grass bank to the right of the footbridge.
1.2	Railway bridge.
1.5	Severn Springs bridge.
2.5	Colwich bridge, (A51).
5	Brindley Bank canal aqueduct, return for short tour.
6	Rugeley bridge, (B5013).
6.5	Railway bridge.
8	Railway bridge, small broken weir above shoot on the right.
8.5	Mavesyn Ridware Footbridge, egress downstream left & portage over the bridge, through the tunnel to reach the canal at Armitage

CANAL

8.5	Launch & paddle North (right).
8.7	Bridge 61.
9.1	Railway bridge.
9.6	Bridge, (A513), Plum Pudding pub, food.
10.2	Bridge 63.
10.3	Bridge 64.
10.6	Mossley bridge 65.
10.7	Bridge.
10.8	Railway bridge.
11	Bridge 66, this is the closest bridge to Rugeley town centre.
11.25	Bridge, (B5013), river bridge 200 metres right.
12	Brindley Bank aqueduct, access for short tour return.
12.25	Bridge
13	Taft bridge.
13.5	Wolsley bridge, (A51).
14.25	Colwich Lock & bridge.
14.4	Railway bridge.
14.6	Little Haywood bridge.
16.4	Great Haywood, finish, two pubs in the village, food, shops.

Long tour (16.2 miles), Great Haywood to Teddesley Park (River Penk) & return.

Short tour (7 miles), Great Haywood to St Thomas's bridge (River Sow) & return.

CANAL

MILES

0	Great Haywood, access from lane. Left off A51 going North through the centre of the village (S/P public footpath, Shugborough Hall). Lane goes under railway then crosses the canal then narrows to a footbridge over the river. Launch just above the lock.
0.2	Great Haywood Junction, turn left under the bridge into Staffs & Worcs canal.
0.5	Cavan's bridge 108, after this bridge the canal widens into Tixall wide, a lake like section almost a mile long. Watch for Kingfishers here.
1.4	Oldhill bridge and lock.
1.6	Tixall bridge.
1.8	Milford aqueduct, canal crosses the river Sow.
2.1	Milford bridge 105.
2.4	Walton bridge 104.
2.7	Stoneford bridge 103.
3	Lodgefield bridge.
3.4	St Thomas's bridge 101, portage point to river Sow for short tour.
3.65	Railway bridge.
3.75	Baswich bridge 100.
4	Meadow bridge 99.
4.2	Radford bridge, (A34), about 1 mile from the centre of Stafford.
5.1	Hazelstrine bridge.
5.4	Deptmore lock.
5.6	Hoseford bridge.
6.1	Acton bridge 93.
6.5	Acton Moat bridge 92.
7	Shutt Hill bridge, Teddesley Park & lock. Portage to river Penk through gate on opposite side of the road.

RIVER

7	Access point for return.
8.5	Acton Trussell bridge.
10.8	Radford bridge, (A34).
11.5	Queensville railway bridge.
11.9	Confluence with the river Sow.
12.2	St Thomas's Priory, island, old left channel silted up keep to main channel.
12.3	St Thomas's bridge, return for short tour.
14.3	Milford aqueduct, canal crosses overhead, low headroom in high water.
14.55	Milford bridge.
16.2	Great Haywood, egress between small weir & footbridge.

RIVER PENK

The river Penk rises in Codsall Wood, near to Wolverhampton and flows North via Coven and Penkridge to join the river Sow to the East of Stafford.

It's beginnings are urban but once it reaches the countryside it cleans up after a few miles. It has a ruling grade of 0/1 and can be an interesting paddle for a group of improvers in medium water but can be a drag in low water. The Staffs and Worcestershire canal shares the same valley and so comes within portagable distance every now and then.

N.R.A. RATING 2   **O/S MAP No: 127**

MILES

0	Clewley, canal aqueduct, from here to Penkridge the river may be too dry in the summer. Access after the tunnel.
0.7	Road bridge.
1	Motor way bridge, (M54).
3	Bridge.
3.3	Coven bridge, unclassified road left off A449 4 miles North of Wolverhampton. Access from field by the bridge.
3.5	Saredon Brook joins from the right, (see Saredon guide). Access through farmyard ask for consent on the day.
3.8	Mill stream leaves to the right, main stream bears left.
3.9	Bridge.
4.2	Bridges, rapid under, mill stream joins from the right.
5	Brewood bridge.
5.5	Minor road comes close, possible access.
6.2	Bridge, (A5), small weir after, nice for playing.
6.4	Lowford bridge, small rapid under.
8	Beacon Hill, access, road close by.
9.1	Cuttlestone bridge, access downstream left bank, friendly farmer.
9.3	Whiston Brook joins from the left.
9.7	Bridge.
9.8	Railway bridge.
9.9	Penkridge bridge, (A449), access from upstream banks.
10.1	Roller Mill (site of), shoot sluices in medium water, inspect in high water. Access downstream right bank.
11.7	Motor way bridge, (M6).
11.9	Teddesley Park, at this point the river and the canal are separated only by the road. Short portage to the canal.
15	Acton Trussel bridges.
17.3	Radford bridge, (A513/A34).
18	Queensville railway bridge.
18.4	Footbridge at the confluence with the river Sow.

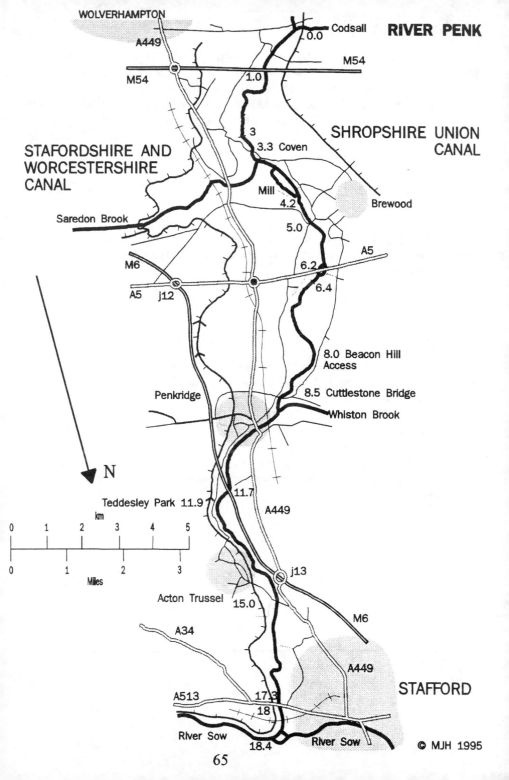

WOLVERHAMPTON

RIVER PENK

Codsall 0.0

M54

A449

M54 1.0

SHROPSHIRE UNION CANAL

3

STAFORDSHIRE AND WORCESTERSHIRE CANAL

3.3 Coven

Mill

Brewood

Saredon Brook

4.2

5.0

A5

6.2

M6

6.4

A5 j12

8.0 Beacon Hill Access

8.5 Cuttlestone Bridge

Penkridge

Whiston Brook

N

11.7

Teddesley Park 11.9

A449

km

0   1   2   3   4   5

j13

Acton Trussel 15.0

M6

0   1   2   3

Miles

A34

A449

A513

17.3

STAFFORD

18

River Sow

River Sow

18.4

© MJH 1995

65

SAREDON BROOK

Saredon Brook rises near to Great Wyrley, much of it's route mirrors the Staffordshire and Worcestershire canal. It flows through Great Saredon & Sandeford to join the river Penk near to Coven to the near of Wolverhampton.

It can be canoed from Saredon Mill in medium water, this is a small river with many sections being tight and narrow, it flows over a gravel bed & is grade 0/1 throughout but rise to grade 2 in flood. It's wooded valley has much wildlife but the channel can get blocked by debris, not the cleanest of rivers but an interesting paddle.

N.R.A. RATING 3   **O/S MAP No: 127**

MILES

0	Bridge, (A460), access downstream left bank.
0.6	Canal feeder weir, 1 metres vertical, can be shot in the centre but angle boat sideways as pool is short.
1	Bridge, road and canal access.
2	Great Saredon Mill.
2.2	Bridge, rapid under.
2.7	Calf Heath bridge, weir under, access after barbed wire fence, parking in marina car park.
2.8	Private road bridge and canal aqueduct.
3.4	Deepmore farm bridge, access on the right bank.
3.8	Weir, shoot in the centre.
4.2	Tunnel under railway, <u>BEWARE</u>, rail across entrance has only 1.3 metre clearance Rapid, weir and rocks in tunnel but plenty of light.
4.6	Sandeford bridge, (A449), <u>BEWARE</u>, pipe across after the bridge, duck under or portage right. Access down bank by the bridge, alternative start for a river Penk tour.
5.5	Confluence with the river Penk at 3.5 Miles.

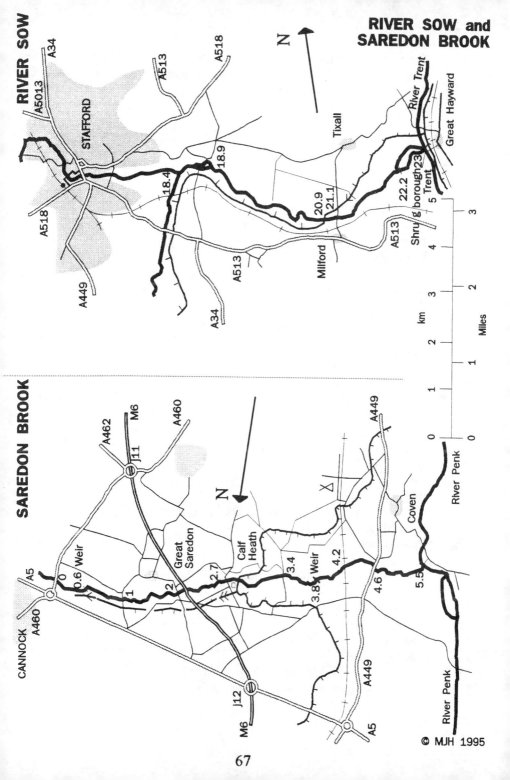

RIVER SOW

RIVER SOW and SAREDON BROOK

SAREDON BROOK

© MJH 1995

67

RIVER ANKER

The river Anker rises out of farmland near to Wolvey in Warwickshire. It then flows Northwest through Nuneaton & Atherstone to join the river Tame under the walls of Tamworth Castle. This is rural river with a ruling grade of 0/1 but has a few weirs along the way. The upper parts may be too shallow in the summer months.

N.R.A. RATING 2   O/S MAP No: 139/140

MILES

0	Woodford bridge. Access, turn right off the A5 one miles after Atherstone, S/P Hartshill, access by the bridge.
1	Footbridge, <u>LOW HEADROOM MUST BE PORTAGED.</u>
1.3	Witherley bridge, (A5), small weir by the bridge.
1.8	Weir, shoot on the right but watch the towback.
2.6	Ratcliffe bridge.
2.9	River Sence joins from the right. This river flows out of Charnwood Forest, it is canoeable from Shakerstone but is shallow & narrow for most of it's route. It has a number of weirs, some sections may be blocked by weed in summer.
3	Weir, 1 metre high, sloping face on the left, vertical slot on the right. Safe in most states.
3.3	Fieldon bridge, (B4116).
4.3	Coventry Canal short portage from left bank.
4.8	Grendon weir, the river is funnelled into a sluice, just before the sluice (which is normally dry), the weir lets the river flow off to the left through a gap in the wall. Care is needed on the approach but the weir can be shot in most states. Difficult portage over private ground.
4.9	Grendon bridge, (B5000).
5.2	Bridge.
6.8	Railway bridge.
7.5	Polesworth bridge, small shoot just above the bridge. Access from upstream left bank, car park.
8.2	Railway bridge.
8.7	Bridge, (M42).
9.2	Alvecote Lakes, three lakes joined by short stretches of river, first two lakes, left bank is the shortest route.
10.2	Shuttington bridge.
10.4	Third lake, keep to the right bank for the shortest route.
13.4	Railway bridge just by Tamworth Low Level Station.
13.9	Railway bridge.
14	Bridge, (A51), Access from public park downstream left.
14.4	Lady Bridge, confluence with the river tame at 27.8 miles, car park, town on right.

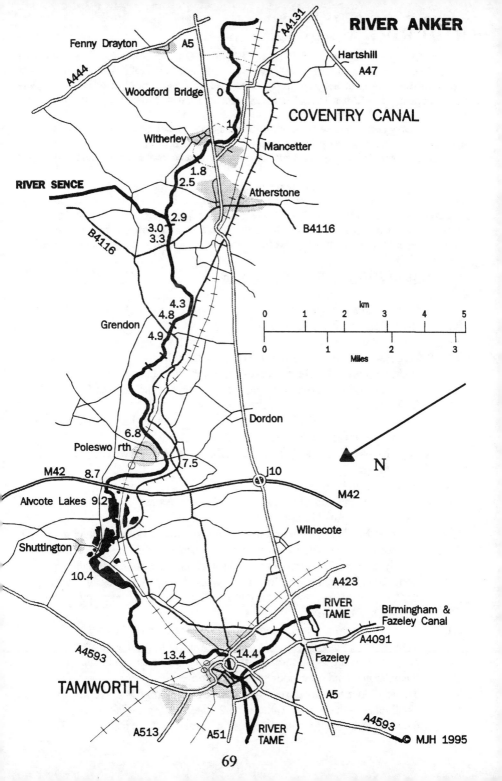

RIVER ANKER

Fenny Drayton

A5

A4444

Woodford Bridge   0

A4131

Hartshill
A47

COVENTRY CANAL

1

Witherley

Mancetter

RIVER SENCE

1.8
2.5

Atherstone

2.9

B4116

3.0
3.3

B4116

4.3
4.8

Grendon

4.9

km

0   1   2   3   4   5

0   1   2   3

Miles

Dordon

6.8

Poleswo rth

7.5

M42   8.7

j10

M42

Alvcote Lakes 9.2

Wilnecote

Shuttington

10.4

A423

RIVER
TAME

Birmingham &
Fazeley Canal

A4091

13.4   14.4

Fazeley

A4593

TAMWORTH

A5

A4593

A513   A51   RIVER
TAME

© MJH 1995

N

RIVER REA (BIRMINGHAM)

The river Rea runs off Windmill Hill by Clent and flows for 11 miles across Birmingham to reach it's confluence with the river Tame near to Gravelly Hill. This is a heavily urbanised river and form Belgrave road is contained in a deep brick culvert with a slightly dished bottom. This "Urban Gorge" was built around 1930 when building work in the town became affected by flooding.

Heavy rain will raise the level of the river very quickly so care must be taken when planning a trip, the leader must keep a keen eye out for debris or the channel being blocked by scaffolding or other building works. Plastic boats are a must as there are many scraped along the way.

The water level indicator by the bridge in Dog Pool lane can be used to estimate the water level for a tour. If the water is touching the bottom of the marker a good run can be expected from Cartland Road but if it is lower it may be better to put in at Second Avenue. If the water is above the first mark there will be no dry "beaches" in the urban gorge & so great care must be exercised, there can be no egress from the urban gorge and so a high water run must not be taken lightly.

N.R.A. RATING 2 to 5.4 miles, 3 after.   O/S MAP No: 139

MILES

0	Cartland Road bridge.
0.1	River Bourne joins from the left.
0.6	Weir, 600mm high.
0.9	Dog Pool Lane bridge, water level marker far left.
1.5	Weir, with projecting bricks, best on the right but can be a scrape.
1.6	Weir, by footbridge, 300mm high. Access from Second Avenue.
1.8	Small weir, run next section on the right.
1.9	Small drop just before Bourne Brook drops in from the left, there are a series of small weirs as the river passes by Cannon Hill Park.
2.5	Weir 1 metre high, watch for raised brick in centre, Followed by Edgbaston Road bridge.
2.8	Edward Road bridge.
2.9	Small Chute in Calthorpe park, "Urban Gorge" begins.
3.1	Balsall Heath Road bridge.
3.3	Belgrave Road bridge, numerous road bridges follow but no problems.
4.3	Duddeston Manor Tunnel, three tunnels to choose from, the centre one is usually the best. Too narrow to turn around and dark but not usually obstructed, it is 600 metres long and has a gentle chute at the end.
5.4	Saltley Viaduct drop and chute. Followed by tunnel under new spine road.
5.9	Aston Church Road.
6.1	Turn corner into a tunnel, hit chute, then another, then out into the light heading for a pillar which has a standing wave in front of it, forward momentum will get you through. If necessary the leader can break out behind the pillar and fend off canoes as they emerge.
6.6	Tunnel, 200 metres long, road built over existing gorge brickwork.
6.8	Confluence with the river Tame at 12.2 miles, best egress is to carry on down the river Tame for 2.5 miles to egress at Tameside Drive just off A452.

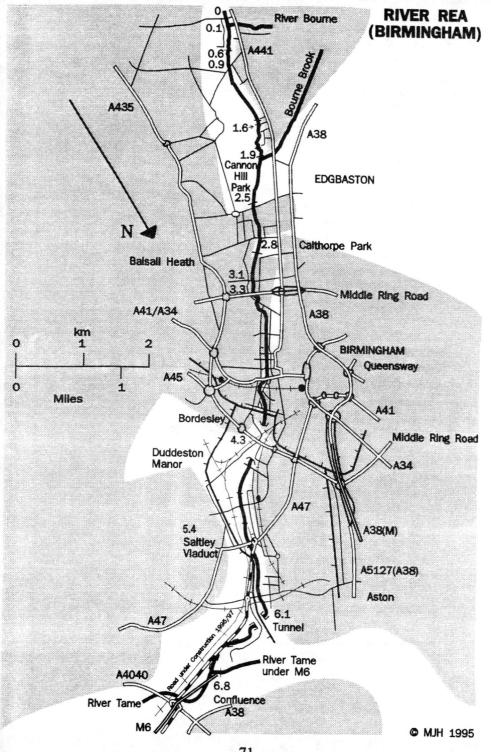

RIVER REA
(BIRMINGHAM)

River Bourne

A441

Bourne Brook

A435

A38

1.6→

1.9
Cannon
Hill
Park
2.5

EDGBASTON

N

2.8   Calthorpe Park

Balsall Heath

3.1
3.3   Middle Ring Road

A41/A34

A38

km
0   1   2

BIRMINGHAM
Queensway

A45

0   1
Miles

A41

Bordesley

Middle Ring Road

4.3

A34

Duddeston
Manor

A47

A38(M)

5.4
Saltley
Viaduct

A5127(A38)

Aston

A47

6.1
Tunnel

Road under Construction 1996/97

River Tame
under M6

A4040

6.8
Confluence

River Tame

A38

M6

© MJH 1995

71

RIVER COLE

The river Cole runs off Weatheroak Hill & flows in a North-easterly direction through Shirley, Small Heath, Kingshurst and Coleshill to join the river Blythe nearby. It is possible in high water from Sarehole Mill in the Hall Green district of Birmingham, but Stetchford or Chelmsley Wood are easier. The distance from Sarehole Mill is 15 miles but the first 7 miles are narrow and urbanised. It is grade 0/1 but can be shallow in the summer, it will be best run in wet weather.

S.T. RATING 2   O/S MAP REF: 131

MILES

0	Stetchford bridge, (A4040), pipe, foot and road bridges. Access down upstream right bank, parking awkward.
1.1	Bridge, low headroom.
1.2	Bridge, Cole Hall Lane, no access.
1.9	Packington Avenue.
2.3	Mill channel leaves right.
2.8	Footbridge, (Bob's Mill).
3.1	Mill channel joins right.
3.8	Bridge, Cooks Lane.
4.4	Low Brook joins from the right.
4.5	Bridge, Moor End Avenue, river is now in a public park.
4.6	Bridge, (A452), river is still in a park from here until the motor way bridge.
4.9	Motor way bridge, (M6).
5.4	Pipe bridge.
5.7	Coleshill Hall Farm bridge, (B4114), ford in 100 metres but access no advisable due to unfriendly farmer, proceed quickly and quietly by.
6.8	Bridge.
7.1	Bridge, (M42).
7.3	Pipe bridge.
7.5	Bridge, (A446).
7.6	Concrete pipe bridge.
7.8	Coleshill bridge, (B4117), egress both upstream banks, river is in a public park. **THIS IS THE LAST PRACTICAL EGRESS**, there is little or no road access until Lee Marston bridges on the river Tame, a distance of 4.5 miles from this point.
9.6	Confluence with the river Blythe.
10.6	Confluence with the river Tame at 19.1 miles.

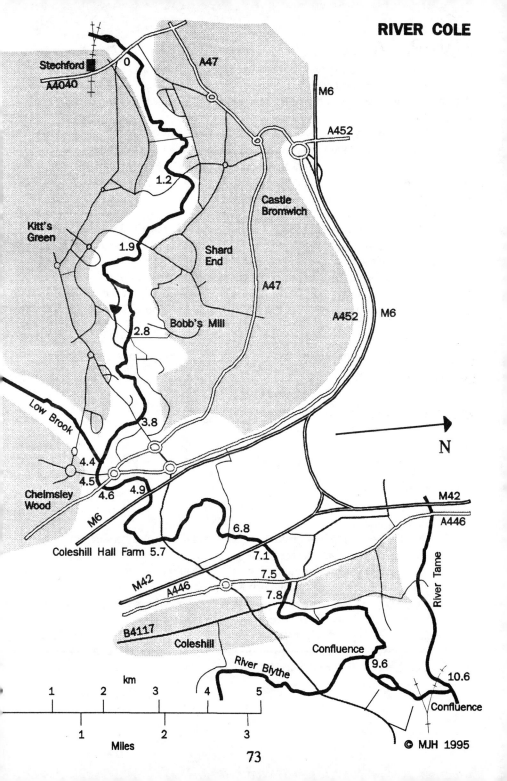

RIVER COLE

Stechford
A4040
0
A47
M6
A452
1.2
Castle
Bromwich
Kitt's
Green
1.9
Shard
End
A47
A452
M6
Bobb's Mill
2.8
Low Brook
3.8
N
4.4
4.5
Chelmsley
Wood
4.6
4.9
M6
6.8
M42
A446
Coleshill Hall Farm 5.7
7.1
River Tame
7.5
M42
A446
7.8
B4117
Coleshill
Confluence
9.6
River Blythe
10.6
Confluence

km
1   2   3   4   5

1   2   3
Miles

73

© MJH 1995

RIVER TAME

The river Tame has two sources, one starts in Monmore Green, Wolverhampton & the other starts in the Oldbury area, they become joined at Bescot Station near to Walsall. The river then flows through Birmingham & Tamworth to join the river Trent by Alrewas.

The upper reaches of this Black Country river flow through ancient metal ore tips as do some of it's tributaries, this makes the river high in heavy metal content. The river has been grossly polluted in the past but has improved over the past 30 years due to the conservation efforts of the water authorities, wildlife has now returned to the upper reaches
fish are now present after Lee Marston.

The middle section (8.9 to 12.2 miles) is not advisable to canoe in anything but low water due to restricted headroom on most bridges and difficult egress due the industrial nature of the area.

The river banks have been heavily engineered as part of a flood control scheme, the baskets used for this make the banks vertical so access points must be chosen in advance. The section through Sandwell Valley is the most pleasant as it flows through park land near to a R.S.P.B. wildlife reserve.

N.R.A. RATING 4 FROM SOURCE TO 22.6 , 3 THEREAFTER
O/S MAP Nos: 128, 139

WOLVERHAMPTON ARM

MILES

0	Bentley Mill Lane bridge, Walsall, access down bank by the bridge.
0.3	Bridge, (A4036).
0.5	Railway bridge.
1.3	Bridge, (A461).
1.5	Railway bridge.
1.7	Confluence with spillway from Oldbury Arm under railway bridge, followed directly by motor way bridge (M6).
1.8	River curves back under motor way and splits into two routes, both routes meet at the confluence with the Oldbury Arm which emerges out of a tunnel. LEFT ROUTE: can be shallow in low water, but is the easiest route in high water. RIGHT ROUTE: this is the most direct route but ends with a tricky left hand bend just by the confluence with the Oldbury Arm especially in high water.
2	Confluence with the Oldbury Arm.

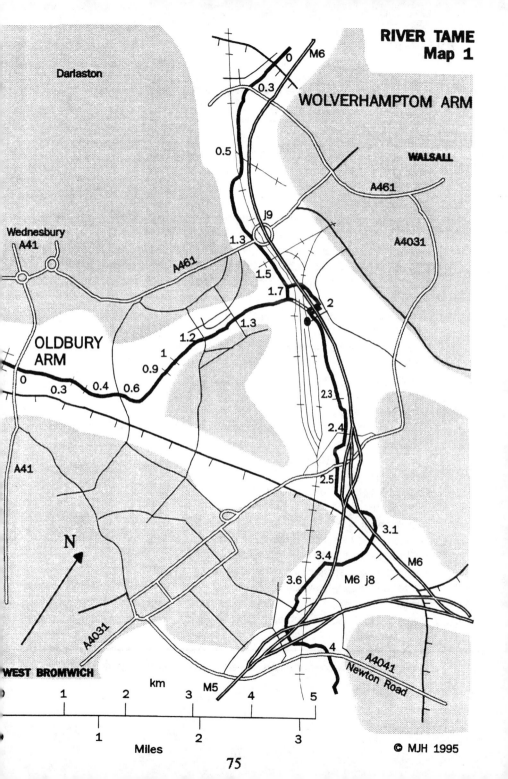

RIVER TAME
Map 1

Darlaston

WOLVERHAMPTOM ARM

WALSALL

A461

Wednesbury
A41

A461

A4031

OLDBURY
ARM

A41

N

WEST BROMWICH

M6 j8

M6

A4041
Newton Road

km

Miles

M5

© MJH 1995

75

OLDBURY ARM

MILES

0	Holloway Bank bridge, (A41), access up stream right over bridge parapet.
0.3	Bridge, river enters a park.
0.4	Weir, 60cm, shoot in the centre.
0.6	Bridge, Hydes Road.
0.9	Weir, shoot between right hand pillar and the bank.
1	Low pipe, this will require a portage in med/high water.
1.2	Bridge, Crankhall.
1.3	Park Hill bridge.
1.7	Spillway going left to the Wolverhampton Arm, LAND HERE TO INSPECT NEXT SECTION. This spillway is the only route possible in high water, 60cm weir at the end of the spillway just before the right bend.
1.8	LOW TUNNEL under railway, 50 metres long, only possible in low water. Must be inspected in any conditions, may be blocked by debris. See above for portage.
2	Confluence with the Wolverhampton Arm.
2.1	Bescot Station bridge.
2.3	Flow control pillars, beware of broaching in flood.
2.4	Bridge.
2.5	Bridge, (A4031).
2.6	Bridge, private.
2.7	Three Motor way bridges, (M6).
3.1	Motor way bridge, (M6), followed by aqueduct of the Tame Valley canal, portage left to canal.
3.4	Motor way bridge, (M5 links).
3.6	Railway bridge.
3.7	Bridge, low headroom in flood.
3.8	Three motor way bridge in succession, (M5 links).
3.9	Railway bridge, NO HEADROOM IN FLOOD.
4	Newton Road bridges, old then new, (A4041), access from filed upstream left of old bridge. Easy parking in old roadway.
4.5	Railway bridge, small rapid under. Beginning of R.S.P.B. Sandwell Valley.
4.9	Forge Mill bridge, flow control pillars.
6	Bridge.
6.4	Hamstead bridges, old then new, (B4149), access upstream right bank, car park.
6.8	Railway bridge.
7	Bridge, in public park.
7.2	Bridge, with flow control pillars just after. Access into car park upstream left.

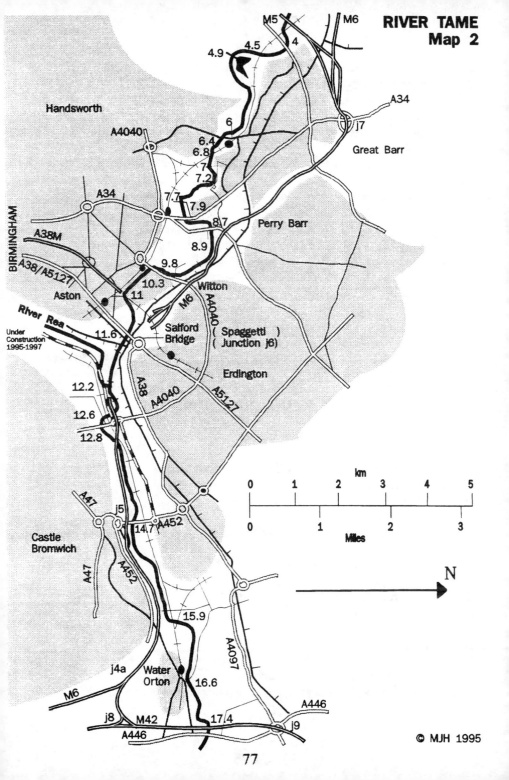

RIVER TAME
Map 2

© MJH 1995

77

7.7	Bridge, small weir just after, near to One Stop Shopping centre. Car parks.
7.9	Perry Barr bridge, (A34), no egress here.
8.7	Perry bridges, old then new, (A453). Access upstream left into old roadway.
8.9	Tame Bridge Industrial Estate, access point up slope on the right into estate road, nice quiet place at weekends.
9.3	Bridge.
9.8	Bridge, access into Holford Industrial Estate, Tame Valley canal 200 metres left.
10.3	Witton bridge, river bends to the left under the bridge which has a shallow arch. Beware of being washed under the arch, best headroom in the centre.
10.9	Bridge.
11	The river flows under and close to the Aston Expressway (A38M).
11.5	Salford bridge, (A38/A5127), upstream left portage to the Tame Valley canal.
11.6	Canal bridge, **BEWARE NO HEADROOM IN MED/HIGH WATER** Aston Brook joins from the right just after the bridge.
11.7	Canal bridge, **BEWARE NO HEADROOM IN MED/HIGH WATER.**
11.8	Pipe bridge, **BEWARE NO HEADROOM IN MED/HIGH WATER.** After this the river flows under the M6 Motor way for approx. 1 mile.
12	Bridge, **BEWARE NO HEADROOM IN MED/HIGH WATER.**
12.2	Rea weir, metal footbridge above, **ALWAYS INSPECT**, this is a stepped weir withside walls, it has large tow back in med/high water. To portage land on the left bank 200 metres above the weir to put back in just below the weir River Rea joins from the right in 50 metres, (see Rea guide).
12.4	Bridge.
12.6	Four bridges, M6, Heartlands Spine Road, railway, then road.
12.8	Bridge, (A4040), rapid under.
13.2	Bridge, the river runs under the motor way again here.
14.7	Bridge, (A452).
15.7	Bridge.
15.9	Railway bridge.
16.6	Water Orton bridge, access from both upstream banks, downstream left is the outflow from Minworth water treatment works, this usually makes the river very foamy for a while. The outflow is treated but it doesn't look good to the author.
17.4	Bridge, (M42).
17.5	Curdworth bridge, (A446), access upstream left bank.
17.6	Railway bridge.
17.8	Bridge.
18.3	Bridge.
18.4	Culvert joins from the left.
18.6	Three bridges in succession, two road, one railway.
19.1	River Blythe joins from the right. See rivers Cole & Blythe guides.

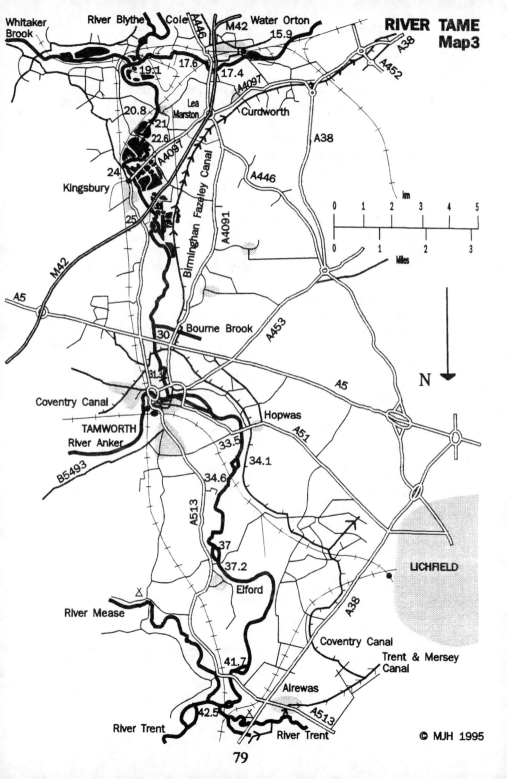

RIVER TAME
Map3

79

19.3	Whitaker Brook, joins from the right.
20.7	Railway bridge.
20.8	Lee Marston bridge.
21	Lee Marston Barrage, this collects floating debris, there may be floating debris backed upstream from the barrage. Portage left past the barrage into the left of the two settlement lakes, keep left. At the end of the lakes there are three weirs, non are safe and are marked with chain buoys.
22.6	Coton Hall bridges, the weir mentioned above are 20 metres above these bridges, all weir channels join up in 100 metres. The best portage is to follow the left side of the left hand lake until just by the first weir, portage through gate, across the road and get in just after the bridge.
24	Kingsbury Mill bridge, (A4097).
25	Bridge, (M42).
25.1	Kingsbury Water Park, Access by prior arrangement only.
30	Two Gates bridge, Bourne Brook joins from the left just before the bridge.
30.4	Aqueduct, Coventry Canal.
31.3	Bridge, (A5), Tamworth by pass.
31.5	Tamworth ring road.
31.7	Metal footbridge, access point, left into public car park (20p). Jolly Sailor pub.
31.8	River Anker joins from the right just before Lady Bridge, after the bridge there are two routes.
	RIGHT ROUTE, along mill stream to weir just by the paper mill.
	LEFT ROUTE, is over the weir and on down the main channel, portage right.
32.1	Tamworth ring road over both routes.
33.5	Hopwas bridge, (A51). Portage to canal.
34.1	Island.
34.6	Railway bridge.
37	Elford Mill.
37.2	Elford bridge.
41.7	Salters bridge, (A513), island.
42.3	Railway bridge and island.
42.5	Confluence with the river Trent at 39.2 miles.

RIVER CHURNET

The river Churnet runs off Bareley Hill and flows into Tittesworth Reservoir, upon leaving it takes a circular route around Leek and goes on to Cheddleton, Alton to join the river Dove near to Rocester.

The Churnet flows through old industrial sites, as many of the factories have now gone it is much cleaner, the Frogall area is the dirtiest but the river cleans up afterwards.

It is canoeable from just under the famous flint mill at Cheddleton, shortly afterwards it combines with the Caldon Canal for a mile or so. The ruling grade is 0/1 but there is a small gorge section that is grade 2/3 with water. There are few weirs, most are safe. The river can be an enjoyable paddle but will be tediously shallow in the summer. Best paddled October to March, a circular tour is possible between Consall and Frogall which includes the gorge section to return on the canal.

N.R.A. RATING 3 from Cheddleton, 2 thereafter

O/S MAP REF: 118,127

MILES

0	Cheddleton bridge, (A520), access into river from pub car park, downstream right, the Caldon canal runs on the other side of the pub.
0.2	Bridge.
0.3	Measuring weir, good play stop.
0.4	Footbridge.
0.5	Footbridge.
0.7	Bridge.
0.9	Bridge.
1.9	Footbridge.
2.1	Caldon canal joins from lock gates on the right.
3.1	Consall Forge, the canal leaves to the left, the river flows over a new dam and sluice gate ahead, this is not shootable. Best portage is to follow the canal for a few metres just before the footbridge, carry down the bank and put in to the left of the dam. The Black Lion Inn good beer and food, good lunch stop.
3.3	Bridge.
3.8	Gorge and rocky fall, this is at a point where the river is funnelled between a rock face and the railway embankment, not recommended for glass fibre boats. The fall is best shot from left to right down an obvious ledge depending on the

water level. Portage is difficult as it is a one at a time procedure down the left bank.

4.1	Railway bridge.
4.4	Railway bridge.
4.9	Railway bridge.
5	Frogall bridge, (A52), the river flows between factories before the bridge.
5.1	Frogall weir, the weir runs at an angle across the river.
5.2	Railway bridge.
7	Farm bridge.
8.3	Railway bridge.
8.8	Oakamoor weir and bridge, the weir is only a few metres above the bridge, it not shootable due to it being shallow at the foot. Egress upstream left bank just before the weir.
9	Railway bridge, from the last bridge to here the river is contained in walls & flows quite fast. Dimmingsdale Y.H.A. hostel half a mile.
9.8	Bridge.
10.1	Smeltingmill bridge.
10.4	Weir, 1 metre high, vertical plunge into a pool.
10.9	Alton bridge.
11.3	Bridge.
11.5	Footbridge.
11.7	Bridge.
11.9	Railway bridge followed by a footbridge.
12	River divides.
12.2	River joins up and flows over Prestwood weir, inspect in all states.
13.1	Denstone bridge, (B5032).
14.3	Bridge, (B5031), and footbridge.
14.5	Bridge, (B5030).
14.7	Rocester bridge and weir, , there is a metal footbridge just before the bridge, the weir is 25 metres after the bridge, it has a 300mm vertical drop onto a 30 degree slope of some 6 metres length, shoot anywhere but inspect in high water Access upstream right of the bridge.
16.1	Bridge.
16.2	Confluence with the river Dove, egress at bridge 300 metres downstream of the confluence.

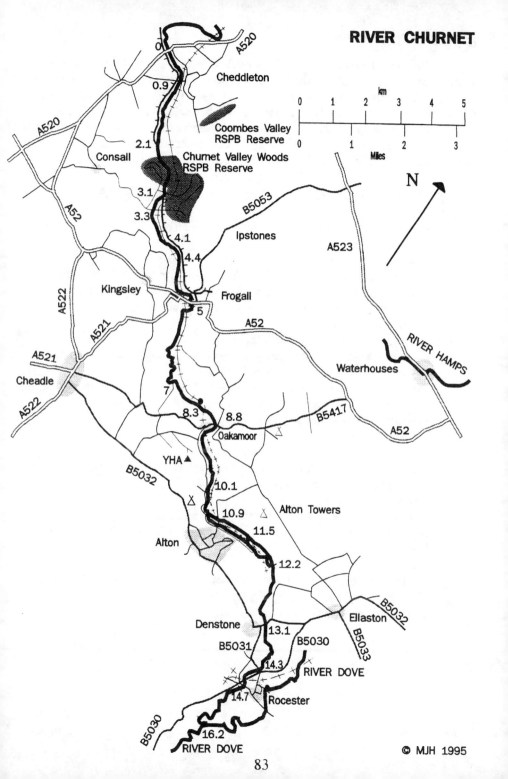

RIVER CHURNET

Cheddleton

Coombes Valley
RSPB Reserve

Churnet Valley Woods
RSPB Reserve

Consall

Ipstones

Kingsley

Frogall

Cheadle

Waterhouses

RIVER HAMPS

Oakamoor

YHA

Alton Towers

Alton

Denstone

Ellaston

RIVER DOVE

Rocester

RIVER DOVE

© MJH 1995

RIVER DOVE

The river Dove runs off Axe Edge by the village of Flash, it then runs in a South-westerly direction through Astonfield. It then proceeds through the famous tourist area of Dovedale, after this the river runs slowly in a wide valley by Ashbourne, Uttoxeter, Sudbury and Tutbury to join the river Trent at Newton Solney near to Burton-on-Trent.

The Dove is controlled by an access agreement due to strong fishing interests. Access details can be obtained from B.C.U. local access officer (S.A.E. please). The section that is normally canoed is the part between Tutbury and the confluence, which is, unfortunately not the most interesting part of the river.

N.R.A. 1A to Rocester, 1B thereafter   O/S MAP REF: 120

MILES

0	Aston bridge, Sudbury, (A515), access upstream right bank by arrangement.
0.5	Railway bridge.
4	Foston Brook joins from the left.
5	Tutbury weir, large weir, half metre drop onto a 6 metre 30 degree slope, best shoot down fish pass approximately 12 metres from the right hand end, it's hard to spot until you are close up but is self centring and good fun.
5.7	Old railway bridge.
5.75	Tutbury bridge, (A50), access by parking in Tutbury Mill Park (height restriction at entrance), park and portage down site of old railway track to the bridge at 5.7.
7.3	Marston bridge, access down bank by the bridge.
7.5	Marston weir, gauging weir with shallow "V" profile, good play spot in low/med water but has very large tow back in high water & so must be inspected.
8.1	Demolished railway bridge, just stone piers in the river.
8.5	Railway bridge.
10	Clay Mills weir, derelict, approach in the centre of the river in low/med water, the weir is covered in high water, take care by broken sluices at the right end.
10.4	Hilton Brook joins from the left.
11.1	Monks bridge,(A38).
11.2	Old Monks bridge, egress downstream right into old roadway.
11.3	Aqueduct, Trent & Mersey Canal, NO HEADROOM, in high water, portage upstream right up bank to canal.
11.7	Railway bridge.
12.7	Confluence with the river Trent at 50.5 miles. Egress onto common land by Newton Solney, follow the B5008 from Burton on Trent, then take Trent Lane opposite Brick makers Arms to the river.

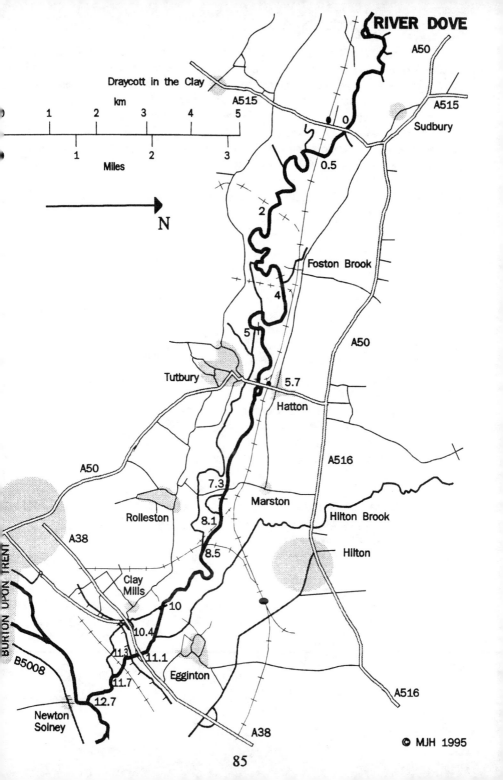

RIVER DOVE

A50

Draycott in the Clay

A515

A515

Sudbury

km

0

0.5

2

Foston Brook

4

5

A50

Tutbury

5.7

Hatton

A516

7.3

Marston

8.1

Rolleston

Hilton Brook

8.5

Hilton

A38

Clay Mills

10

10.4

11.3

11.1

11.7

Egginton

12.7

Newton Solney

A516

A38

© MJH 1995

BURTON UPON TRENT

B5008

N

RIVER MANIFOLD

The river Manifold runs off Axe Edge not far from the village of Flash near to the source of the river Dove. It flows in a Southerly direction through Hulme End, after which it enters it's gorge overlooked by the famous Thor's Cave, upon reaching Ilam it has just a short run to join the river Dove near to Dovedale. This river can probably only be paddled in the winter and then only after good rainfall, as there are various fissures leading to subterranean streams the river has the habit of disappearing completely in the summer. The land that it flows through is mostly private and some National Trust, it is important to ask permission. Grade 1/3 depending on water level, it runs over a rocky bed and so is rarely flat and doesn't give much time to relax. The best indicator is a ford on Hoo Brook at GR 095 560, the water must be 4" deep running over the ford before the river is paddlable.

N.R.A. RATING 1A   O/S MAP No: 128

MILES

0	Ecton, access from lay-by near to village.
0.4	Old railway bridge.
0.8	Ecton bridge.
1.5	The Lee, alternative access and parking.
3	Wetton Mill bridge, access, parking and camping.. Confluence of Hoo Brook.
3.2	Bridge and ford.
4.3	Weags bridge, Access and Parking.
4.5	River Hamps joins from the right.
6	Weir, inspect, shootable.
6.8	Weir, inspect, shootable.
7.7	Rushley farm bridge.
7.8	Footbridge.
8.8	Bridge. Access Ilam Y.H.A. Hostel half a mile.
9	Ilam bridge, egress downstream left.
9.3	Weir, inspect in high water,
9.7	Confluence with river Dove.

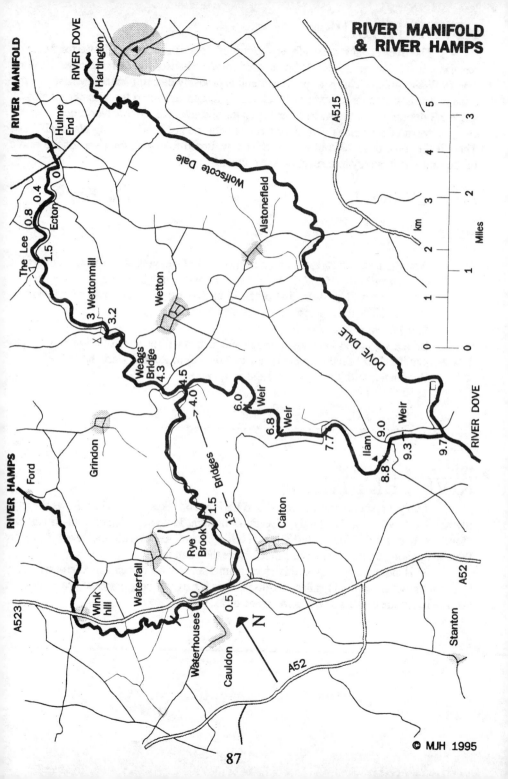

RIVER MANIFOLD
& RIVER HAMPS

© MJH 1995

87

RIVER HAMPS

The river Hamps starts life as a group of streams running off Butterton Moor, it remains a small river all it's life. It flows through Waterhouses to reach the river Manifold near to Weags bridge. This is a spate river and is probably best run actually whilst it is still raining, it is a winter/spring river as it can totally disappear during the summer months. A grade 2/3 depending on the water level the major obstacles will be tree blockages.

Most of the land is owned by farmers with the last 2 miles being National Trust. There is the track of an old railway which is now a road following the river for the whole of the valley so it is easy to inspect prior to running.

N.R.A. RATING 1B   O/S MAP No:

MILES

0	Waterhouses, car park, 100 metres West of Village on A523, Access from here.
0.5	Greensides bridge, (A523), the river drops and you will enter a very steep sided, narrow valley. This is the first of the 13 bridges crossing the river, we will not mention all of them unless they have significance.
1.5	River Rye joins from the left.
4	Bridge 12, egress here and portage 400 metres left for weags bridge or go on to join the river Manifold, next egress in 2.6 miles at Rushley Farm bridge.
4.1	Confluence with the river Manifold at 4.5 miles.

RIVER BLYTHE

Many streams are catchmented into Earleswood lakes, from which flows the river Blythe. It flows in a Northerly direction through Knowle, Hampton-in-Arden and Stonebridge it then skirts Coleshill to reach it's confluence with the river Tame by Whitaker picking up the river Cole 1 mile before the confluence.

It is possible to canoe this river from Hampton-in-Arden but there are many fishing interests along it's 11 miles. because of this it may not be a practical proposition. It has a ruling grade of 0/1 and a N.R.A. grade of 2.